Dear Rashida,
You are blessed
and highly favored.
Lilly P. Crook
12-12-20

Inspiring Thoughts

- 2nd Edition -

Your life journey is a reflection of choices.

- Lilly Pearl Crook -

ISBN 13: 978-1-7334966-2-9

Published by Relasonship LLC
Dacula, GA 30019.

Printed in the USA.

Dedication:

I dedicate this second devotional book to a number of individuals including; my three children, Belicia, Omawumi, and Elihu, the love of my life, Phillip Igbinadolor, and my dear father, Mack Wilbert Crook, Sr.

Belicia, Omawumi, and Elihu

You guys give me real purpose. I love you from my soul and you all share the space in my heart that is preserved for greatness. I am so sorry that your father doesn't share this earthly space with us anymore, but I am confident that when he left this earth, he opened his eyes to Jesus. He is in the best place ever and I am sure he is just another angel watching over the three of you.

I am your ride or die mom. I will always love and protect you in prayer. The three of you motivate hope in my soul and encourage me to feel hope through my heart. It is with the deepest form of love that I dedicate this book filled with my personal thoughts to the three of you. I am blessed with enough wisdom and knowledge to express my thoughts in ways that motivate many. I continue to be spiritually motivated by the Holy Spirit, and I am humanly motivated by the unexplainable feeling of being a mom. You three are my earthly jewels and I am blessed to walk the earth with you and to have you acknowledge me as your mom. I wish you all peace, love, happiness, discernment, forgiveness, patience, understanding and love. You three are truly gifts from God; I wish you all things that are good.

Phillip Igbinadolor

My dearest love, I will always love you. You will always be a love sitting in my heart forever. I only remember the good times and I remember how deep we once loved. I remember feeling like I was the only woman on this earth when we were together. I remember you holding my hands after we married and telling me that you would love me forever. Phillip, you kept your promise; you loved me until you took your last breath and I still feel your presence and love. It is because of your love that I am a confident woman, a woman that understands the depth of real love. I thank you for fathering our three children. I pray that you are watching over them and talking to Jesus about how special they are to us. I dedicate this book of loving thoughts to our memory and our love.

Mack Wilbert Crook, Sr.

To my beautiful and wonderful father who I still miss tremendously after 35 years of him passing. I only have loving memories of our relationship. I understood your weaknesses and I never allowed your weaknesses to taint the love that was glued to my heart for you. I focused on the good in you and that was easy because your heart and soul were good. I thank you for being courageous enough to father ten children, even when others thought it was foolish. I thank you for loving my mother without conditions and for leaving her with a heart filled with love for you forever. I thank you for believing in me and encouraging me to love Phillip deeply. I know you and Phillip are dancing around Heaven. Dad, I am still making you and the love of your life proud.

Introduction:

The Book of Proverbs has always inspired me to pursue greatness. Greatness for me is having a heart that is focused on service with a humble spirit. My life experiences have taught me that wisdom is earned, and it requires a God-centered heart. I am honored that God allowed my heart to be inspired by the wisdom of the Book of Proverbs.

I am not sure how many devotional books I will publish, but I am sure that this book will be one of my personal favorites. The biblical verses in the Book of Proverbs allowed me to express my innermost self without hesitation. The verses took me down a journey like no other. I discovered that wisdom is to be appreciated by the wise and unwise, secured inside your heart, and sheltered from evil forces. Wisdom is a blessing for those who know they are highly favored. The verses in the Book of Proverbs are sometimes raw and are a direct reflection of Jesus. I was reintroduced to the power and commitment of Jesus, our Lord and Savior, through the truth expressed in life lessons.

Your personal responses to this devotional book of inspiring thoughts are welcomed.
Please email the author at hopeandinspiration55@gmail.com.

For more details, please visit the author's website at
www.hopeandinspiration.squarespace.com.

- January -

If wisdom makes you arrogant, you are misguided.

- January 1 -

Fear of the Lord is the foundation of true knowledge,
but fools despise wisdom and discipline.
Proverbs 1:7

Author's Thoughts:

It is impossible to fear God without a degree of wisdom. Wisdom clears out the heart to allow us to acknowledge and respond to the needs and concerns of the poor. When we refuse to consult with God, we are rejecting wisdom. When we miss one opportunity to represent righteousness, another opportunity is waiting. God stands by our side, even when we turn our backs to discipline. He is waiting for us to acknowledge His presence.

Reader's Thoughts:

- January 2 -

My child, listen when your father corrects you.
Don't neglect your mother's instruction.
What you learn from them will crown you with grace
and be a chain of honor around your neck.
Proverbs 1:8-9

Author's Thoughts:

I pray for the young and for the old, but my deepest prayers are for the young. The world's definition of right and wrong seems to be changing with each generation. Even Christians have made adjustments to accommodate the world's view of right and wrong. God's word doesn't change, His word is clear, and His expectations are firm. I pray that the elders embrace the young and take advantage of teaching the young Christ-like values. Let your teaching be a chain of honor for the young.

Reader's Thoughts:

- January 3 -

My child, if sinners entice you, turn your back on them!

Proverbs 1:10

Author's Thoughts:

Do not let the power of darkness reign in your heart. If darkness reigns in your heart, it will control your life journey. We all have dark experiences in our life journey, but Jesus died on the cross to give us an opportunity to forgive and to be forgiven. Embrace the sacrifice that was poured out for you. Turn your back to sin. Jesus is the light, stay in the light with Him. His grace is sufficient.

Reader's Thoughts:

- January 4 -

Such is the fate of all who are greedy for money; it robs them of life.

Proverbs 1:19

Author's Thoughts:

I had the experience of living with someone for many years who had a remarkable greed for money. I witnessed his greed journey and monitored the ups and downs. The end result was that he had no financial security. His greed journey motivated an attitude of never being content.

God blesses us even more when we are thankful and content with where he chooses to place us in life. Greed can quickly become an idol, any idol other than God, can quickly move us away from God's presence.

Reader's Thoughts:

- January 5 -

How long, you simpletons, will you insist on being simpleminded?
How long will you mockers relish your mocking?
How long will you fools hate knowledge?
Proverbs 1:22

Author's Thoughts:

Some associate humbleness with being naive. I do not think those who are humble are simpleminded. In fact, I think those who are humble are more apt to be wise. Humble people are listeners and learners. Humble people speak profoundly. Humble people do not favor attention. Humble people appreciate service. Foolish people think they are the wisest and the most knowledgeable. Foolish people never open their hearts to learning from the humble.

Reader's Thoughts:

- January 6 -

Come and listen to my counsel. I'll share my heart with you and make you wise.

Proverbs 1:23

Author's Thoughts:

Listening to God's heart requires an intimate relationship. For me, it involves meditation in a quiet and peaceful place in my heart. It is impossible to make wise decisions without recognizing God's heart and power. Wisdom is recognized by others and is appreciated by most. The word introduces you to the heart of Jesus.

Reader's Thoughts:

- January 7 -

For they hated knowledge and chose not to fear the Lord.

Proverbs 1:29

Author's Thoughts:

Constructive and earned knowledge is not to be measured. Identifying our shortcomings and changing them with guidance from the wise brings us closer to the Holy Spirit. Embracing the Holy Spirit motivates us to release fear. Releasing fear prompts us to embrace our faith. Biblical knowledge opens our souls to freedom.

Reader's Thoughts:

- January 8 -

They rejected my advice and paid no attention when I corrected them.
Therefore, they must eat the bitter fruit of living their own way
choking on their own schemes.
Proverbs I: 30-31

Author's Thoughts:

One can argue that we are choking on our sins in this country. We seem to be more divided than ever. Christians claim to love Jesus, but cannot seem to love their neighbors. We are killing each other like it is a sport. We are demeaning our women as if women are objects. We are not protecting our children. We disrespect our churches and we choose fear over faith. We are rejecting the word; therefore, we are left without armor.

Glory be to God for offering forgiveness and salvation.

Reader's Thoughts:

- January 9 -

But all who listen to me will live in peace, untroubled by fear of harm.

Proverbs 1:33

Author's Thoughts:

I do not quite know how to live in complete peace because fear still, sometimes, overtakes my emotions. I can say that I am on a peace journey. I understand that, for me, I must maintain a continual relationship with God so that I can increase my faith and decrease fear. I look forward to the moment when I make that connection with God that releases all fear. For now, I keep praying, being thankful, praising Him, serving the needy, and keeping hope alive in my soul.

Reader's Thoughts:

- January 10 -

Tune your ears to wisdom and concentrate on understanding.

Proverbs 2:2

Author's Thoughts:

There are many things, good and bad, that happen to me that I do not understand. Sometimes understanding requires me to invest time with Jesus. Oftentimes, my lack of understanding can be attributed to wavering faith. When things happen to me that I cannot wrap understanding around, I find myself in prayer often. Prayer helps me to understand that God's ways are not my ways and His wisdom can't be measured. It is in these times that I trust His plans for my life, even when I do not understand. My heart is open to wisdom, so I focus on understanding.

Reader's Thoughts:

- January 11 -

My child, listen to what I say, and treasure my commands.

Proverbs 2:1

Author's Thoughts:

I find that it is difficult, at times, to listen to God because I struggle with accepting His voice. His voice is straight forward and clear. His word is profound and life changing. His love is undeniable. His commands are designed to set you free. His commitment to righteousness is in the Holy Spirit. His ways are good and perfect. He is almighty. His armor is all around you wherever you go. He stands ready to hear you and He delights when you honor His commands.

Reader's Thoughts:

- January 12 -

Cry out for insight, and ask for understanding.

Proverbs 2:3

Author's Thoughts:

I pray that how I disciple is a true reflection of God's love. In many ways, I write and share as a form of discipleship. I have a desire for biblical awareness and understanding. I have embraced the fact that others look to me for wise insight. I understand the power of words and thoughts. I appreciate the opportunity to share my thoughts with others. I acknowledge how impactful a disciple of Jesus can be and the tremendous responsibility that is involved. I scream out to Jesus often for strength and protection. I ask God for a world with peace, not so much for me, but for the people I love.

Reader's Thoughts:

- January 13 -

For the Lord grants wisdom! From his mouth come knowledge and understanding.

Proverbs 2:6

Author's Thoughts:

If others think we are wise, that's okay. When we start thinking we are wise, we probably need to check our motives. Wisdom is reflected in our words and actions. Wisdom is developed eventually. Wisdom is appreciated by others. Wisdom can be a burden if taken advantage of. God is the giver of wisdom, we should all embrace it and be thankful. Wise people are well respected, but not always well received. Wisdom comes with tremendous responsibility. Honor wisdom well.

Reader's Thoughts:

- January 14 -

He grants a treasure of common sense to the honest.
He is a shield to those who walk with integrity.
Proverbs 2:7

Author's Thoughts:

How often do we confuse foolishness with common sense? Common sense is provided by and treasured by God. Foolishness is normally associated with doing evil things. God protects those with common sense and integrity. God allows fools to be fools. Common sense makes being humble possible. Common sense is a gift from God that protects your thoughts and actions. Thanks be to God for allowing common sense to flow through our hearts and minds.

Reader's Thoughts:

- January 15 -

He guards the paths of the just and protects those who are faithful to him.

Proverbs 2:8

Author's Thoughts:

Please accept the gift of the Holy Spirit! You can wrap your sins and concerns around the Holy Spirit and release all your cares. Allow the Holy Spirit to guide your life and be faithful to the power of the Holy Spirit. Embrace forgiveness and repentance and believe that you are truly forgiven. Accepting God's gift of forgiveness allows you to release your sins to the Holy Spirit. God is faithful and He protects those who are faithful. God gives you an opportunity to always experience love and be hopeful. God is love.

Reader's Thoughts:

- January 16 -

Wise choices will watch over you. Understanding will keep you safe.

Proverbs 2:11

Author's Thoughts:

Your life journey is a reflection of choices. It is important to understand that we all make choices that are not pleasing to God. We are sinners saved by God's grace with an offering of the Holy Spirit. I have learned, through my own choices, that God is standing close even when we fail to consult with Him. He is close by, waiting for us to acknowledge the mistake. Ask for forgiveness, repent, and move on in the Holy Spirit. For those of you who see perfection as a real goal, relax, God is near. Jesus died on the cross because God knew His people would be imperfect. Imperfection causes us to meet up with God more often.

Reader's Thoughts:

- January 17 -

Wisdom will save you from evil people, from those whose words are twisted.

Proverbs 2:12

Author's Thoughts:

I can't say that my words are never twisted, but I can say that God gives me a gentle reminder when my words are inconsistent with love and kindness. Yes, wisdom is a liberator, but wisdom can also save you from your own negative thoughts because wisdom speaks loudly. Wisdom prompts ordinary people to be bold. Evil fears wisdom. It is necessary to embrace wisdom because the devil is offended by wisdom.

Reader's Thoughts:

- January 18 -

Wisdom will save you from the immoral woman,
from the seductive words of the promiscuous woman.
Proverbs 2:16

Author's Thoughts:

In my opinion, good and faithful women are not always appreciated in our society. It seems the definition of a beautiful and loving woman changes with each generation. Women who respect men and are prepared for love are often set aside for immoral women and for women who seem not to apply wisdom to their life choices. Women who love well, but don't mind voicing their boundaries, are wise in my eyes. I think we need to take our power back and never accept disrespect from our men. Never think that being disrespected is acceptable, even if it feels good in the moment.

Reader's Thoughts:

- January 19 -

My child, never forget the things I have taught you.
Store my commands in your heart. If you do this,
you will live many years, and your life will be satisfying.
Proverbs 3:1-2

Author's Thoughts:

In 2017, I dedicated time to a 365-day read of the Bible. Today, November 17, 2018, I am reading day 321 in the Book of Acts. I spent many years depending on others to teach me the Word and I am very thankful to my wonderful teachers, but I am so excited about my personal dedication to the Word. Each morning, during my devotional time, I feel the presence and power of Jesus through the Word. I encourage all of my readers to praise God in their own personal time. Praise Him for life.

Reader's Thoughts:

- January 20 -

Never let loyalty and kindness leave you!
Tie them around your neck as a reminder.
Write them deep within your hearts.
Proverbs 3:3

Author's Thoughts:

Loyalty is necessary. Kindness is shared. This earth is a step-stool to Heaven. Eternity requires loyalty to God's commands. Eternity requires commitment to loving God with all your heart and soul. Eternity requires us to love our neighbors like we love ourselves. Eternity requires acknowledging our sins, asking and receiving forgiveness, and repenting. Eternity requires us to remain hopeful. Eternity requires us to be forgivers. Eternity is available to all of mankind.

Reader's Thoughts:

- January 21 -

Trust in the Lord with all your heart; do not depend on your own understanding.

Proverbs 3:5

Author's Thoughts:

Trusting God, for me, is always evolving. I am not fully committed, but my intentions are always to be fully committed. There are times when my challenges are so intense that I feel like waiting on God is just not possible. In those desperate times, I take the wheel from God and steer alone. God is faithful, He always speaks to me during my weakest moments. My thoughts are redirected in Him and I manage to get back on my faith journey quickly. When you lose your way and get off God's track, please remember that He is a forgiving God.

Reader's Thoughts:

- January 22 -

Seek his will in all you do, and he will show you which path to take.

Proverbs 3:6

Author's Thoughts:

You must open your heart so that God can speak to you; spend quality time seeking God's will. The Bible is God's visible teacher for believers. The Word teaches God's path. The Word encourages you to stay on God's path and it encourages communication with God. God speaks through His immeasurable knowledge and guidance that can only be found in the pages of the Bible.

Study the word and listen to God speak. His path is clear. Be blessed!

Reader's Thoughts:

- January 23 -

Don't be impressed with your own wisdom.
Instead, fear the Lord and turn away from evil.
Proverbs 3:7

Author's Thoughts:

I am reminded throughout the day of God's power. These daily thoughts remind me to fear God. I used to think that fearing God wasn't reachable, but now the fear of God is present in my life. This fear keeps me grounded and aware of His goodness. This fear reminds me that God is the giver of wisdom and He can take it away at any moment. This fear keeps me humble and motivated to share God's gifts with others.

Reader's Thoughts:

- January 24 -

Honor the Lord with your wealth and with the best part of everything you produce.

Proverbs 3:9

Author's Thoughts:

The best parts of me are my children and grandson. I am thankful for the gift of life and for God's trust in me to love and honor these gifts. I can never express how thankful I am for God blessing me with three beautiful and giving children. God didn't have to gift me with such blessings, but He did. We should all focus on goodness and honoring God for life. It is in a state of humbleness that I love God and my family. My wealth is in life giving thoughts.

Reader's Thoughts:

- January 25 -

My child, don't reject the Lord's discipline,
and don't be upset when he corrects you.
Proverbs 3:11

Author's Thoughts:

We are eager to accept "good" gifts from God, but we contest God's discipline. God is a just and fair God. He corrects through discipline and love. He doesn't discriminate in discipline nor does He discriminate when He shares hope and faith. We must all learn to embrace God's discipline and accept His forgiving power. I often recognize God's discipline and pray for acceptance and understanding of His discipline. Those that we discipline are probably inspired by seeing us accept God's discipline with respect.

Reader's Thoughts:

- January 26 -

For the Lord corrects those he loves,
just as a father corrects a child in whom he delights.
Proverbs 3:12

Author's Thoughts:

It seems all too many fathers have failed generations of children by not correcting bad behaviors during crucial developmental ages. It is very possible to correct through loving discipline. We do not have to choose love or discipline. Discipline is effective when the person we are disciplining understands the purpose and still feels the gift of love even when disciplined. Fathers, please don't be intimidated by negative reactions to proper training of your children. Teach them to obey rules and find positive ways to correct disobedience. Fathers who are obedient to God can successfully correct disobedient children.

Reader's Thoughts:

- January 27 -

Joyful is the person who finds wisdom, the one who gains understanding.

Proverbs 3:13

Author's Thoughts:

Amen! I am so thankful for joy. I decided years ago that joy is a gift from God, and I am not giving it back. We all can control what we allow others to bring to our table of joy. Wisdom requires us to be aware of the Holy Spirit and to respond. Your understanding of the Holy Spirit and the power of the Holy Spirit is wisdom.

Joy is appreciated when God blesses you with wisdom.

Reader's Thoughts:

- January 28 -

Wisdom is more precious than rubies;
nothing you desire can compare with her.
Proverbs 3:15

Author's Thoughts:

When others see you as wise, you have the responsibility to fear God and do what is right. You can always regain your sight and open your heart to be refilled by the Holy Spirit. Sharing the love of Jesus and honoring service is a mandate for wisdom. Nothing can compare to wisdom given by God. God given wisdom opens a path for us to be chosen instruments to take and share the Word with others. Oftentimes, our only opportunity to share the love of Jesus is by how we live our faith journeys.

Reader's Thoughts:

- January 29 -

Wisdom is a tree of life to those who embrace her,

happy are those who hold her tightly.

Proverbs 3:18

Author's Thoughts:

God and wisdom are life trees. If we embrace God, it is easier to embrace wisdom. Those who hold wisdom tightly and God close are happy in life moments. Wisdom connects us to Jesus and inspires an intimate relationship with Him. If wisdom isn't displayed in how you live, it is very possible that wisdom escaped your life. If wisdom makes you arrogant, then you are misguided.

Reader's Thoughts:

- January 30 -

My child, don't lose sight of common sense and discernment.
Hang on to them, for they will refresh your soul.
They are like jewels on a necklace.
Proverbs 3:21-22

Author's Thoughts:

I know individuals who live without common sense or discernment. It seems that their lives are train wrecks, but they are not wise enough to acknowledge the train wrecks. If you love someone with poor judgement, there will come a time when all you can do is pray for protection and a change of heart. Only God can take the place of poor judgement and open minds to discernment. We can all use a refresher course in common sense.

Reader's Thoughts:

- January 31 -

Do not withhold good from those who deserve it
when it's in our power to help them.
Proverbs 3:27

Author's Thoughts:

Service is an honor and a gift. I urge you not to withhold your service from others. Honor God in service to the deprived. Honor God in how you love those who are less fortunate. Remember that God created us all, rich and poor, healthy and unhealthy, addicts and non-addicts, abused and not abused. Keep service in your thoughts so that you can honor God through service. Remember that your time is valuable not only to you, but to others as well. Mankind needs to feel your love.

Reader's Thoughts:

- February -

Stop judging others with a less measured view than you judge yourself.

- February 1 -

If you can help your neighbor now, don't say,
"Come back tomorrow, and then I'll help you."
Proverbs 3:28

Author's Thoughts:

View the definition of neighbor as taught in the Bible. We are all neighbors to each other. See that homeless man, woman, and child as your neighbor. See that disabled veteran as your neighbor. See that blind man as your neighbor. See that family member that you haven't spoken with for so long as your neighbor. See that person in prison as your neighbor. Reach out and help your neighbors. Your neighbor's needs are immediate, there is no time to wait until tomorrow.

Reader's Thoughts:

- February 2 -

Don't pick a fight without reason, when no one has done you harm.

Proverbs 3:30

Author's Thoughts:

Stop looking for a reason to be unhappy. Stop being difficult for no valid reason. Stop focusing on the worst in you and others. Stop comparing your life to others. Stop judging others with a less measured view than you judge yourself. Stop enabling others, then get upset with the person you are enabling because they remain the same. Stop worrying and start praying. Stop trying to be God.

Reader's Thoughts:

- February 3 -

Don't envy violent people or copy their ways.

Proverbs 3:31

Author's Thoughts:

Envying violent people and mimicking their ways sounds very much like following the ways of the devil. Violence is not included in God's commands and it contradicts how God expects us to treat our neighbors. It is impossible to assault your neighbor if you live a love-focused life. Violence starts with a thought and it can be controlled with a thought. It is foolish to envy people with violent spirits.

Reader's Thoughts:

- February 4 -

The Lord curses the house of the wicked, but he blesses the home of the upright.

Proverbs 3:33

Author's Thoughts:

Don't confuse suffering with punishment. You and your home can be blessed through a journey of suffering. God will bring you out of suffering and reintroduce you to the Holy Spirit. All of my trials have been and will be defeated. I trust God through all challenges and wonderful times as well. Life, for me, is sometimes a bed of trials, but I rise up each morning and turn my thoughts to God's promises which are always true. My home will not be cursed, I refuse to give into wickedness. Glory be to God!

Reader's Thoughts:

- February 5 -

The Lord mocks the mockers but is gracious to the humble.

Proverbs 3:34

Author's Thoughts:

Never be embarrassed to be humble or to acknowledge your faith to others. God expects us to have humble hearts, hearts filled with love and hope. For the hopeless, believers are expected to be hopeful. For the homeless, believers are expected to love and feed. For the nonbelievers, believers are expected to disciple in love. God is gracious and kind to those who are humble in His word.

Reader's Thoughts:

- February 6 -

My children, listen when your father corrects you.
Pay attention and learn good judgement,
for I am giving you good guidance.
Don't turn away from my instructions.
Proverbs 4:1-2

Author's Thoughts:

God is our heavenly father and He can always be trusted. Our earthly fathers are imperfect and are gifted with the responsibility of teaching. A father's guidance and discipline are immeasurable. Children who turn away from good guidance and disregard what is right will experience a life of challenges that are inconsistent with a life of wisdom. God is standing by waiting for our children to accept and appreciate guidance. It is never too late to accept God's guidance, nor too late to appreciate His discipline.

Reader's Thoughts:

- February 7 -

Get wisdom; develop good judgment.
Don't forget my words or turn away from them.
Proverbs 4:5

Author's Thoughts:

In my opinion, wisdom and good judgment are developed over an impactful journey of studying the word and developing an intimate relationship with God. It requires us to be in the word, pray with vigor, talk with Jesus before making decisions, rely on His armor of protection, praise Jesus in all circumstances, love Jesus with all our hearts and souls, and more. Wisdom and good judgement will wither away without a continual relationship with God.

Reader's Thoughts:

- February 8 -

Getting wisdom is the wisest thing you can do!

And whatever else you do, develop good judgment.

Proverbs 4:7

Author's Thoughts:

How do we acquire wisdom? How do we apply wisdom? How do we maintain wisdom? How do we respect wisdom? How do we identify wisdom? How do we honor wisdom?

Believe in Jesus Christ and you can be saved. Rejoice in your beliefs. Disciple and encourage other believers.

Reader's Thoughts:

- February 9 -

If you prize wisdom, she will make you great.
Embrace her, and she will honor you.
Proverbs 4:8

Author's Thoughts:

Wisdom has honored me for many years. I am thankful that God guides many of my thoughts and that He encourages me to share my thoughts. I am honored and thankful that you are reading my thoughts today. I pray that you are inspired by your God-given thoughts. Embracing wisdom is such a precious journey. Peace be with you always.

Reader's Thoughts:

- February 10 -

Guard your heart above all else, for it determines the course of your life.

Proverbs 4:23

Author's Thoughts:

Allow God in your heart for guidance and protection. The devil is standing by waiting for you to lose faith so that he can enter your heart. You must always be on guard and always keep God close. Only God can protect your heart from the power of the devil. Trust in God's power and not your own. Give God an opportunity to impact the direction of your heart, if you don't, the devil will take His place. Pray vehemently for proper guidance.

Reader's Thoughts:

- February 11 -

Avoid all perverse talk; stay away from corrupt speech.

Proverbs 4:24

Author's Thoughts:

We all have been guilty of engaging in idle talk or rumors. Gossip can be sensational and addicting. Gossiping about other's personal or private affairs is harmful. When I gossip, I must admit, it is never done in love. I find myself in a conversation with others who are gossiping and decide to join the gossip train. I am convicted as soon as I allow it to happen and feel a sense of disappointment. Glory be to God for the Holy Spirit giving gentle reminders when we sin.

Reader's Thoughts:

- February 12 -

Look straight ahead, and fix your eyes on what lies before you.

Proverbs 4:25

Author's Thoughts:

The past is gone and can't be changed. If your thoughts are in the present moment, it can motivate change. What lies before you is always promising. You can affect change now; you can change the direction of your path in each moment. Look forward and make decisions in forward thoughts. Believe that your sins are forgiven and move forward being guided by your belief and faith in Jesus. Don't let old sin become new or continual sin. Fix your eyes on a bright future filled with the Holy Spirit.

Reader's Thoughts:

- February 13 -

Mark out a straight path for your feet; stay on the safe path.

Proverbs 4:26

Author's Thoughts:

I pray that my children are encouraged by the path their father and I took together. We loved each other deeply and protected each other the best way we knew how. We were not always on a safe path, but we clearly understood how important it was to focus on a straight path. We both love Jesus. I pray that our love is reflected in how our children love. I am thankful for the beautiful times in my heart that Phillip and I shared together. He was my forever love and I know without a doubt that I was his forever love. We loved well.

Rest in peace, my love.

Reader's Thoughts:

- February 14 -

Don't get sidetracked; keep your feet from following evil.

Proverbs 4:27

Author's Thoughts:

Evil is obvious. Doing evil and doing good are both choices. In your moment of choice, please consider God's ways. Sin is real, but so is Jesus. Sin is powerful, but God is all powerful. Doing wrong is sometimes easy, but doing right is eternal. Treating our fellow mankind with love and respect is hope. Hope is good and dependable. Love well!

Reader's Thoughts:

- February 15 -

For the lips of an immoral woman are as sweet as honey,
and her mouth is smoother than oil.
Proverbs 5:3

Author's Thoughts:

It seems, at times, that the idea of a moral woman has changed. In this context, I am simply referring to the world's view of a moral woman. God's views of a moral woman will never change.

Is a woman honorable if she follows the desires of her heart? Does a moral woman express herself through body displays? Do moral women want sexual pleasures? Do moral women express thoughts that contradict their husbands?

Just giving you questions to develop thoughts.

Reader's Thoughts:

- February 16 -

Let your wife be a fountain of blessings for you.

Rejoice in the wife of your youth.

Proverbs 5:18

Author's Thoughts:

Men please view your wives as blessings. It is difficult not to love, honor, and respect a blessing. Rejoicing in your wife not only pleases your wife, but more importantly, it pleases God. A man that cherishes the position of head of a household is a man that pleases God. A man that embraces the responsibilities of a husband is a man that gratifies God. A man that honors God and lives a life that is reflective of God's word is a man that delights God. A man that is prepared to give up his life for his wife and children is a man that satisfies God. Women be thankful for your man of God.

Reader's Thoughts:

- February 17 -

For the Lord sees clearly what a man does,
examining every path he takes.
Proverbs 5:21

Author's Thoughts:

It can be a bit intimidating knowing that the Lord sees you and your actions clearly. It can also be encouraging because with that knowing, God is also watching over you. He is prepared to acknowledge and honor your commitment to the Holy Spirit and your commitment to the word. God's all-knowing power is a blessing to the world and a doorway to eternity. Let your paths be attractive to God.

Reader's Thoughts:

- February 18 -

An evil man is held captive by his own sins;
they are ropes that catch and hold him.
Proverbs 5:22

Author's Thoughts:

Imagine being tied down with a rope every time you sin without a way out. Jesus died on a cross and rose again so that your "sin ropes" can be released. You never have to be tied down again. Accept His releasing power and forgiveness. His power and your relationship with Him will change how you view these ropes. In Jesus, there is freedom, freedom from all sin. We are given the blood and body of Jesus so that we can be released from sin. Accepting and being committed to God's unchanging hands is a choice.

Reader's Thoughts:

- February 19 -

He will die for lack of self-control;
he will be lost because of great foolishness.
Proverbs 5:23

Author's Thoughts:

Self-control is necessary for an intimate relationship with God. Your decisions to make good or bad choices are determined by self-control. An absence of self-control can lead you down a journey of destruction that can only be stopped with God-focused self-control. Foolishness is born out of the lack of self-control. Foolish decisions and actions are a gift to the lack of control. The shortage of self-control creates inconsistency in our faith journey.

Reader's Thoughts:

- February 20 -

But the man who commits adultery is an utter fool,
for he destroys himself.
Proverbs 6:32

Author's Thoughts:

Adultery is a threat to family and a treat to the self-confidence of the one who commits adultery. Adultery causes immense pain for immediate family members and the victim of adultery. Being faithful in marriage is expected of children of God. Adultery can destroy the most complete marriages. When a man or woman commits adultery, he or she violates the entire family, children, grandchildren, aunts, uncles, and grandparents. Everyone is violated. All are affected because of the destructive nature of adultery. Christians should speak on adultery and hold men and women in the church who are committing adultery accountable.

Reader's Thoughts:

- February 21 -

So don't bother correcting mockers; they will only hate you.
But correct the wise, and they will love you.
Proverbs 9:8

Author's Thoughts:

Mockers are pleased when they cause pain to others. People who are wise are pleased to see love flow in the hearts of others. Mockers are quick to hate. People who are wise look for reasons to love. Mockers will encourage wrong behavior. Wise people encourage and praise good behavior. Let God change mockers and don't let the mockers impact your faith journey in negative ways.

Reader's Thoughts:

- February 22 -

The godly are showered with blessings;
the words of the wicked conceal violent intentions.
Proverbs 10:6

Author's Thoughts:

Worthy discernment will reveal the wicked and is a characteristic of believers that are incalculable. If you lack the ability to judge well, immoral people can talk you into thinking that their actions are good instead of revealing their true intentions. Focus on the godly and pray for discernment. God will reveal the true actions of the wicked.

Reader's Thoughts:

- February 23 -

Love wisdom like a sister; make insight a beloved member of your family.

Proverbs 7:4

Author's Thoughts:

It takes the quietness of a peaceful place to embrace insight that can be applied to our daily lives. True wisdom and insight are gifts from God through the Holy Spirit. It takes prayer, meditation, and a desire to understand the word to acknowledge and maintain wisdom and insight. We need to fall in love with the wisdom and insight that can only come from God. Worldly wisdom and insight will confuse your thoughts and have a negative impact on your faith. Allow the Holy Spirit to enter your thoughts so that God-given wisdom and insight will impact your ways and words.

Reader's Thoughts:

- February 24 -

Follow my advice, my son; always treasure my commands.

Proverbs 7:1

Author's Thoughts:

God's commands are clear.

God's commands are treasured by all but followed by few.

God's commands are of God.

God's commands are attainable through the Holy Spirit.

God's commands are realistic.

God's commands are to be honored.

God expects Christians to honor and treasure His commands.

Reader's Thoughts:

- February 25 -

Obey my commands and live!

Guard my instructions as you guard your own eyes.

Proverbs 7:2

Author's Thoughts:

Just think about how important your eyes are to your body. Would you take a sharp object and puncture your eyes? Apply this to God's commands. If you wouldn't cause harm to or disrespect your eyes, then why would you not guard God's commands and apply His commands in your life? It is God who gave you your eyes and it is God who gave us His commands. God expects us to obey His commands and live a life of peace filled with joy.

Reader's Thoughts:

- February 26 -

Listen as Wisdom calls out! Hear as understanding raises her voice!

Proverbs 8:1

Author's Thoughts:

Listen to the wisdom of God. God's voice works through our conscience. Your conscience speaks to you before all decisions. Your conscience is designed to voice good into your mind so that your decisions are of God. I have made too many mistakes because I chose not to listen to God's gentle voice. Our lives would be more fruitful if we accept and act on the moments God gives us before the decision. Wisdom calls out before the action. God forgives after the action, but forgiveness requires action on your part. You will meet God less often in forgiveness, if you listen to His voice before your actions.

Reader's Thoughts:

- February 27 -

My advice is wholesome. There is nothing devious or crooked in it.

Proverbs 8:8

Author's Thoughts:

Don't be fooled by ungodly advice. Sometimes people wrap advice in a pretty bow and make it seem like gold when it is really poisonous. Wholesome advice is good and sensible. It is well thought out and inspired by the word. It sometimes challenges your heart because it is contrary to what you expect to hear. It comes from a place of love and it is constructive. It faces truth head on and turns its back on untruth. Listen to the wise and be thankful for the gift of wisdom.

Reader's Thoughts:

- February 28 -

My words are plain to anyone with understanding,
clear to those with knowledge.
Proverbs 8:9

Author's Thoughts:

I sometimes struggle to understand God's words because the words seem too powerful for me to comprehend. I have found that the more I read God's word, the more I understand God's ways. I yearn to understand God's teachings and His commands. I have no doubt that God will continue to enlighten me as I stay on my faith journey. I am comfortable with the knowledge and wisdom God has blessed me with in this moment and I look forward to His blessing of knowledge in the next moment. God's words are clear in that love is of the utmost importance.

Reader's Thoughts:

Reader's Thoughts:

March

Joy is promised to those who love Jesus and honor His ways.

- March 1 -

For wisdom is far more valuable than rubies.
Nothing you desire can compare with it.
Proverbs 8:11

Author's Thoughts:

God determines your level of wisdom. The world is impacted by wisdom that can only come from God. It appears that, oftentimes our leaders operate on their own manmade wisdom without even consulting with the word. It appears that some Christians, who are powerful with decision making authority, make decisions that are contrary to the word of God. If we Christians can stand by the word under challenging conditions and decisions, we can encourage others to explore Christianity. We acquaint others with God by how we live.

Reader's Thoughts:

- March 2 -

Common sense and success belong to me.
Insight and strength are mine.
Proverbs 8:14

Author's Thoughts:

Embrace common sense and success. Accept insight from God and hold on to His strength. These are all gifts from God. Let common sense humble your soul so that you can live an impactful life. In difficult times, be a reflection of strength. Use insight to discipline yourself and to disciple others. God is generous in common sense, success, insight, and strength, but they all come with tremendous responsibilities. Respect these gifts and God will continue to allow you to be impactful on His behalf.

Reader's Thoughts:

- March 3 -

"And so, my children, listen to me for all who follow my ways are joyful."

Proverbs 8:32

Author's Thoughts:

You will find joy in an intimate relationship with God. You can hold onto and experience joy even when you are managing extremely difficult challenges. Keep your mind tuned into God and your thoughts connected to the word. Joy is a beautiful gift from God and God doesn't expect you to return joy to Him unused. You make choices each moment, include the choice to experience joy in each moment. Listen to God speak to you through the word and enjoy life in joy.

Reader's Thoughts:

- March 4 -

Joyful are those who listen to me,
watching for me daily at my gates,
waiting for me outside my home!
Proverbs 8:34

Author's Thoughts:

Listening to God's gentle words are pleasing to our souls. Listening to Him influences our hearts to love. Closing our hearts to God's gentle words leads to confusion and unwise decisions. Pray and ask God for guidance and endurance to overcome all obstacles. Be prepared to be tested through all obstacles, but know that God will give you the strength to endure all things and leave you with a joyful heart. God is always close.

Reader's Thoughts:

- March 5 -

"Leave your simple ways behind, and begin to live;
learn to use good judgement."
Proverbs 9:6

Author's Thoughts:

We are all guilty of using poor judgement with no intention of consulting with God before we make decisions. Your ways will always be simple if you act without or before conversing with God. Our lives are hindered when we make decisions that impact our lives without listening to God's gentle guidance. Learning to use good judgement requires quality time in the word and a continual relationship with Jesus.

Reader's Thoughts:

- March 6 -

Instruct the wise, and they will be even wiser.
Teach the righteous, and they will learn even more.
Proverbs 9:9

Author's Thoughts:

Others will express their views on your wisdom. It is humbling when others think you are wise and you don't. Those who think they are not wise seem to get wiser during the progression of their faith journey. A humble and righteous person is a priceless gift to his or her faith community. A humble, wise, and righteous person is clearly gifted by the Holy Spirit. Your fellow mankind needs to see images of Jesus as a welcome mat to righteousness.

Reader's Thoughts:

- March 7 -

"For whoever finds me finds life and receives favor from the Lord. But those who miss me injure themselves. All who hate me love death."

Proverbs 8:35-36

Author's Thoughts:

I feel and experience God's favor every moment of my life. He holds me up when I am falling. He speaks to me before I offend with words. He listens to my prayers. He comforts me in distress. He motivates me to remain hopeful. He extends His mercy and grace at all times and He loves me unconditionally. God's favor is available, live in ways that you won't miss His favor.

Reader's Thoughts:

- March 8 -

Fear of the Lord is the foundation of wisdom.
Knowledge of the Holy One results in good judgment.
Proverbs 9:10

Author's Thoughts:

Fearing the Lord is healthy and positive. God is all knowing, He is worthy of our fears. Fearing God motivates us to live in His commands and to accept His discipline. Fearing the Lord creates a solid spiritual foundation for us to worship and praise Jesus. Fearing the Lord encourages our minds to focus on the goodness of the Lord. Wisdom is available to those who fear the Lord and remain faithful to the word. Visiting the word often enhances our ability to make decisions based on good judgement.

Reader's Thoughts:

- March 9 -

If you become wise, you will be the one to benefit.

If you scorn wisdom, you will be the one to suffer.

Proverbs 9:12

Author's Thoughts:

Yes, we all have scorned wisdom and yes, we all have suffered because of the scorn. The journey to wisdom is not straight, but it is worth the ups and downs. The benefits of wisdom impact future generations. All generations need to identify with wise people as examples. It is beneficial to witness wisdom played out by people we respect and love. God is in the middle of wisdom. He grants wisdom to those who love Him and His ways.

Reader's Thoughts:

- March 10 -

A wise child brings joy to a father;
a foolish child brings grief to a mother.
Proverbs 10:1

Author's Thoughts:

It is amazing to witness foolish children become wise. A mother's grief is turned into joy when she experiences the switch from foolish decisions to wise decisions. Fathers are relieved as they witness the journey of wise children. If your child is in the "foolish" stage, please keep encouraging them and trust in the power of prayer. God can change a foolish heart into a wise heart in a moment. Be patient and inspire the foolish.

Reader's Thoughts:

- March 11 -

Tainted wealth has no lasting value, but right living can save your life.

Proverbs 10:2

Author's Thoughts:

It seems that human power, influence, and money are ruling the world, but are the furthest from God's truth. God can humble and change the position of the powerful in an instant. The powerful have no power over God. God is fair and faithful to His word. Keep living according to the word and watch God save your soul. Joy is promised to those who love Jesus and serve His ways.

Reader's Thoughts:

- March 12 -

The Lord will not let the godly go hungry,
but he refuses to satisfy the craving of the wicked.
Proverbs 10:3

Author's Thoughts:

God has never let me hunger for hope, love, or His mercy. I feel His presence at all times and I no longer question His love. He has blessed me in that He provides an abundance of His people on earth to love and protect me. He also brought home to heaven angels to protect me and my family. I am pleased with God.

Reader's Thoughts:

- March 13 -

Lazy people are soon poor; hard workers get rich.

Proverbs 10:4

Author's Thoughts:

It is tough for me to speak about the results of being lazy, because I am uncomfortable being lazy. I do know that hard work is rewarding. I know that hard work leads to richness beyond monetary value. Hard work gives you a sense of peace and security. Hard work motivates me to meditate in the word and to appreciate my relationship with Jesus Christ.

Reader's Thoughts:

- March 14 -

The wise are glad to be instructed, but babbling fools fall flat on their faces.

Proverbs 10:8

Author's Thoughts:

There are times when I am a "babbling fool." I contest God's ways and do things my way, but I am wise enough to identify and respect God's consequences for my rebellion. I have learned to ask for forgiveness, accept forgiveness, and be better. I love God's teachings and I acknowledge that I am a sinner in need of God's grace and mercy. I now embrace wisdom because I clearly understand that wisdom can exist without perfection.

Reader's Thoughts:

- March 15 -

People with integrity walk safely,
but those who follow crooked paths will be exposed.
Proverbs 10:9

Author's Thoughts:

We all have slipped and fallen in our faith and we will slip and fall in the future. Keep holding onto integrity and your falls will be few. Our thoughts can lead us to crooked thinking and our thinking can lead us to challenge our integrity. Control your thoughts through a Christ-focused life and visit the word often. Keep walking safely, stay on a straight path, guard your integrity, and communicate with Jesus.

Reader's Thoughts:

- March 16 -

The words of the godly are a life-giving fountain;
the words of the wicked conceal violent intentions.
Proverbs 10:11

Author's Thoughts:

You must be wise enough to identify and move away from the wicked. The company you keep and what you allow your ears to hear impacts your actions. Stay close to godly people and godly things. People who speak godly words and live godly lives are disciples. Pay attention to how disciples live and how they worship. The wicked are real and are guided by evil, believe their words and actions, and act accordingly. In order to be godly, you must move away from sin and accept Jesus' life-giving commands.

Reader's Thoughts:

- March 17 -

Hatred stirs up quarrels, but love makes up for all offenses.

Proverbs 10:12

Author's Thoughts:

Love solves all problems. If you love, as Jesus commands, you will never wrong your fellow mankind. Love always results in Christ like ways and decisions. If we love our enemies, we will not do them harm. If we love our neighbors, we will treat them with kindness. If we love our sisters and brothers, we will not encourage wrong. If we love our parents, we will not continue to make decisions that causes them pain. If we love our spouses, we will not violate them. If we love Jesus, we will follow His commands.

Reader's Thoughts:

- March 18 -

Wise words come from the lips of people with understanding,
but those lacking sense will be beaten with a rod,
Proverbs 10:13

Author's Thoughts:

For me, it is clear, I am inconsistent with wisdom through words and thoughts. Sometimes wisdom is applied and other times I speak without any consideration for wisdom. In those weak moments, I quickly acknowledge, ask for forgiveness, and move on to change. We should never beat ourselves up for inconsistency, but instead work closer with God to change. God knows all things, He understands your weaknesses. The faithful are resilient.

Reader's Thoughts:

- March 19 -

Wise people treasure knowledge, but the babbling of a fool invites disaster.

Proverbs 10:14

Author's Thoughts:

Treasuring knowledge has been a challenge for me, but I have grown in knowledge throughout my life. I learned to accept and evaluate good advice even if it is difficult to hear. The more I meditate on the word, the more accepting I am of constructive advice. The word helps me identify and treasure valuable knowledge. As I age, I am less foolish and a bit wiser.

Reader's Thoughts:

- March 20 -

The wealth of the rich is their fortress;
the poverty of the poor is their destruction.
Proverbs 10:15

Author's Thoughts:

Since I became an adult and could work for pay, God has provided all my needs. I must say, my needs are few and I appreciate abundance. As a child growing up, I can remember my needs not being met. There were times I needed clothes, times I needed food, times I needed heat to warm my body, and times I needed a ride home from track practice. Those times of need prepared me for times of abundance. I know how it feels to be poor and I know how it feels to have abundance. I am thankful for all times.

Reader's Thoughts:

- March 21 -

People who accept discipline are on the pathway to life,
but those who ignore correction will go astray.
Proverbs 10:17

Author's Thoughts:

The gift of accepting discipline is immeasurable. I am sure all of us can remember times, recently, when we were guilty of not accepting God's discipline and I am sure that we acknowledged the significance of nonacceptance. We are all guilty of going astray, going astray sometimes reminds us of God's forgiving power. Our life journey is full of ups and downs but believing and knowing Jesus encourages us to be thankful for our journey. God is love even when we disregard His teaching and discipline.

Reader's Thoughts:

- March 22 -

Hiding hatred makes you a liar; slandering others makes you a fool.

Proverbs 10:18

Author's Thoughts:

Hatred is destructive on all levels and to all who hate. Knowing Jesus makes it difficult to hate; following Jesus' ways makes it impossible to hate. God gives us a loving and forgiving spirit through the Holy Spirit. The Holy Spirit doesn't slander others. The Holy Spirit doesn't hate its neighbor. The Holy Spirit encourages and motivates love. Those who are foolish disregard the Holy Spirit. Hate is an enemy to the spirit of Jesus Christ.

Reader's Thoughts:

- March 23 -

Too much talk leads to sin. Be sensible and keep your mouth shut.

Proverbs 10:19

Author's Thoughts:

Heavenly father teach me to keep my mouth closed before I sin with my words. Our words are sometimes our most challenging sin. We must learn to meditate on the word and on our words. Our words can tear down or uplift. Too often, we tear down with our words that include Jesus in our sentences. Jesus is a loving and forgiving God. We can all learn from the depth of His love. Jesus' words are fair and just. Jesus' words are hopeful and motivate peace. God lives in us so that our thoughts and words are pleasing to Him.

Reader's Thoughts:

- March 24 -

The words of the godly encourage many,
but fools are destroyed by their lack of common sense.
Proverbs 10:21

Author's Thoughts:

I am thankful that my words can be words of wisdom and encouraging to others. God blessed me with a thought process that can be motivating, that motivating thought process used to intimidate me, but it no longer does. I have learned to share and embrace my own thoughts that are sometimes inspired by the Holy Spirit. The flip side is that I am not always in control of my emotions and thoughts, so common sense is evaded at times. It is in those moments that I regret speaking foolishly. I take that regret to God and ask for forgiveness.

Reader's Thoughts:

- March 25 -

When the storms of life come, the wicked are whirled away,
but the godly have a lasting foundation.
Proverbs 10:25

Author's Thoughts:

I am an example of weathering storms and an image of a lasting foundation. Storms of life should be expected for all mankind. Jesus died on the cross for our sins. Why should we expect not to have trials? Trials keep us face to face with Jesus Christ. Trials reminds us of the need to pray. Trials bring our faith full circle when we find ourselves safely through the trials. Trials remind us of Jesus' sacrifice. We should all embrace our trials in the same way we embrace our gifts.

Reader's Thoughts:

- March 26 -

Lazy people irritate their employers, like vinegar to the teeth or smoke in the eyes.

Proverbs 10:26

Author's Thoughts:

Lazy is a term and action that offends me. I have always worked hard to accomplish goals and to complete tasks. My parents taught me the value of hard work and integrity. My experiences with lazy people are all experiences that I care not to remember. Lazy people will ride your back, jump off, and take credit for the ride. Lazy people don't mind letting others pull their weight. It is difficult for a lazy person to value integrity. Staying in our faith journey requires commitment and diligence, there is absolutely no room for complacency.

Reader's Thoughts:

- March 27 -

The hopes of the godly result in happiness,
but the expectations of the wicked come to nothing.
Proverbs 10:28

Author's Thoughts:

Hope is powerful and it requires a positive thought process. Hope is available to all mankind. Hope and belief in the unseen Jesus Christ is an unexplainable gift. Jesus can be trusted with your hope. He will turn hope into a beautiful reality. Rely and trust in God's expectations and in your own expectations. Goodness and hope can fulfill your expectations of Jesus.

Reader's Thoughts:

- March 28 -

Honesty guides good people; dishonesty destroys treacherous people.

Proverbs 11:3

Author's Thoughts:

It appears that some Christians in American have blurred the lines between honesty and dishonesty. It seems our standards and expectations of our leaders have been lowered and we accept dishonesty wrapped in an ugly bow. We even go so far as to defend dishonesty. Non-believers are watching how we defend and fight for dishonest leaders. It is probably time for all Christians to stand up for right and stop supporting wrong. Why can't we call out wrong for what it is and not try to comfort those who are dishonest? Dishonesty can destroy a nation.

Reader's Thoughts:

- March 29 -

The godly are directed by honesty; the wicked fall beneath their load of sin.

Proverbs 11:5

Author's Thoughts:

We move through life experiencing honesty and sometimes dishonesty in our actions. None of us are immune from sin; we are all capable of being dishonest. The good news is that God saves and Jesus forgives. God's salvation saves you from falling and staying in the sin of dishonesty. Dishonesty is the proximate cause of many sins. It is possible to be guided by honesty, just jump on the train with Jesus as the conductor. Jesus opens your heart to love, hope, forgiveness, peace and joy, which puts sin at a distance.

Reader's Thoughts:

- March 30 -

The godly are rescued from trouble, and it falls on the wicked instead.

Proverbs 11:8

Author's Thoughts:

It is ungodly to wish trouble on anyone. When you are rescued from trouble or survive trouble, tell someone about God's power. All sinners, including you and I, need to witness God's forgiveness through one that has been forgiven. It is possible to have many trials, but not be troubled. A troubled soul is a gift to the devil.

Reader's Thoughts:

- March 31 -

It is foolish to belittle one's neighbor; a sensible person keeps quiet.

Proverbs 11:12

Author's Thoughts:

I am a firm believer that love trumps evil. Instead of responding to an unkind act with an unkind action, try responding with love and kindness. If you are unable to respond with love, then consider being quiet. Some actions from others do not require a response. If you must respond, exercise godly control.

Reader's Thoughts:

~ April ~

Lazy people will ride your back, jump off, and take credit for the ride.

- April 1 -

A gossip goes around telling secrets,
but those who are trust worthy can keep a confidence.
Proverbs 11:13

Author's Thoughts:

It is extremely important to have someone that you can share your innermost thoughts, your gifts, and your pain with. Finding a godly person that is worthy of your trust is to be cherished. We all should acknowledge gossip and remove ourselves from the conversation. Gossip is another word for lie. A gossiper never gets the facts correct because the facts are of no interest to a gossiper and the gossiper can't be trusted with facts.

Reader's Thoughts:

- April 2 -

Without wise leadership, a nation falls; there is safety in having many advisers.

Proverbs 11:14

Author's Thoughts:

Good leaders select really decent advisers to help them lead. Good leaders listen to and respect their advisers. Good leaders take immediate action when a dishonest adviser is discovered. Good leaders respect others. Good leaders' words are measured. Good leaders understand and respect their positions. Good leaders know the impact their decisions and choices have on the people they lead. Good leaders are wise and know the source of their wisdom. Families fall without godly leadership.

Reader's Thoughts:

- April 3 -

There's danger in putting up security for a stranger's debt;
it's safer not to guarantee another person's debt.
Proverbs 11:15

Author's Thoughts:

My youngest brother, Willie, gave me excellent advice many years ago and I apply his advice to my decision making. He advised me to never loan anyone money or valuables that you can't afford to give, or you want returned. In most cases, if someone needs you as security, that someone probably mismanaged God's gifts. How can you expect to be paid back by someone who is irresponsible and mismanage their own money? I learned not to respond quickly to a request for financial help, but to allow a thought process and prayer before responding.

Reader's Thoughts:

- April 4 -

The Lord detests people with crooked hearts,
but he delights in those with integrity.
Proverbs 11:20

Author's Thoughts:

I absolutely love people with rock solid integrity. When my son, Elihu, went to college at UGA, my advice to him was to guard his integrity. Integrity is connected to your heart. If your heart is not pure, impurity will come from your actions and words. God is so pleased with men and women that exhibit rock solid integrity because they humble themselves to the gospel. Integrity determines the nature of your faith.

Reader's Thoughts:

- April 5 -

A beautiful woman who lacks discretion is like a gold ring in a pig's snout.

Proverbs 11:22

Author's Thoughts:

All women are beautiful in God's eyes. Women should honor their beauty by embracing wisdom and using discretion in their actions and words. A holy woman is such a wonderful gift from God to her husband and children. It is important for a man to have a partner who is rooted in faith and understands the power of forgiveness. I am saddened by the high divorce rate in America. Women have the power to have a positive impact on divorce rates. We as women must learn to use God's weapons against the devil and not worldly weapons. Release the chains that are choking our families.

Reader's Thoughts:

- April 6 -

If you search for good, you will find favor,
but if you search for evil, it will find you!
Proverbs 11:27

Author's Thoughts:

Finding God's favor is freedom. Accepting God's authority builds you up and gives you power to defeat sin. Good and evil cannot reside in the same heart. We must choose which one we will embrace each moment. If you find yourself faced with evil, look around for the good. It is possible that God sent you to be the good for others. Stop boasting about your strengths and try boasting about your weaknesses. Mankind needs to see examples of mankind relying on God's strength and not their own.

Reader's Thoughts:

- April 7 -

Trust in your money and down you go! But the godly flourish like leaves in spring.

Proverbs 11:28

Author's Thoughts:

I don't understand or know how it feels to trust in money because I don't remember a time when money was that important to me. God has provided enough for survival and I am thankful. I trust that God will always provide. My focus is on living a faith journey that makes Jesus smile and to be thankful for His grace and mercy. I am confident that all things turn out for the good with Christ.

Reader's Thoughts:

- April 8 -

The wise don't make a show of their knowledge,
but fools broadcast their foolishness.
Proverbs 12:23

Author's Thoughts:

It takes wisdom not to showcase the knowledge that is gifted to you by God. God promises knowledge to all His people. The level of knowledge and wisdom is different for each of us. In my opinion, the best way to impact people is to live a Christ-like life for others to witness. You can broadcast foolishness or wisdom through your actions. God is always observing and so is mankind.

Reader's Thoughts:

- April 9 -

Wickedness never brings stability, but the godly have deep roots.

Proverbs 12:3

Author's Thoughts:

Keep your faith deeply rooted in godly ways. Faith that is not rooted can be easily shaken. The devil can uproot your faith if you don't pay attention to the word and apply the word to how you live. Deep rooted faith brings stability and a will to rely on God's grace and mercy.

Reader's Thoughts:

- April 10 -

A worthy wife is a crown for her husband,
but a disgraceful woman is like cancer in his bones.
Proverbs 12:4

Author's Thoughts:

Husbands should respect the worthiness of their wives. A lack of respect and love can create a disgraceful woman. A worthy woman can become cancer to her husband's soul if she is not treated in godly ways by her husband. Men are powerful, how they use that power can determine the worthiness of their wives.

Reader's Thoughts:

- April 11 -

Better to be an ordinary person with a servant
than to be self-important but have no food.
Proverbs 12:9

Author's Thoughts:

I appreciate ordinary people because Jesus lived an ordinary life. Jesus balanced His power with an ordinary life. It is impossible to be a disciple if you are self-absorbed. In order to disciple, you must be of service to others and have a selfless heart. The people you serve become more important than a self-centered attitude. Sincere service removes self-first thoughts and replaces them with unselfish thoughts.

Reader's Thoughts:

- April 12 -

Work hard and become a leader; be lazy and become a slave.

Proverbs 12:24

Author's Thoughts:

Your faith journey requires attention. The moment you don't acknowledge or nourish your faith is when the devil arrives. Your covenant with Jesus is fulfilled through your faith. There is nothing more important than knowing and understanding why you have this faith journey. Your faith in Jesus makes you right with God. Do not become a slave to the world, but instead become a slave to your faith. Jesus Christ already freed you from the penalty of sin. Glory be to God!

Reader's Thoughts:

- April 13 -

Thieves are jealous of each other's loot,

but the godly are well rooted and bear their own fruit.

Proverbs 12:12

Author's Thoughts:

Bearing fruit is discipleship. God expects us to disciple others. As Christians we are required to introduce others to the love of Christ. It is pleasing when Christians reach nonbelievers through teaching the word and through their own faith journey. It is life changing when others want to know God because of how you live your faith journey. Faith is an action word and nonbelievers watch the actions of believers.

Reader's Thoughts:

- April 14 -

Wise words bring many benefits, and hard work brings rewards.

Proverbs 12:14

Author's Thoughts:

Wise words followed by Christ-like actions is music to God's ears. God will reward you for your commitment to fulfilling the law through your faith in Jesus Christ. His rewards are true and immeasurable. His rewards impact future generations. Your faith in Jesus Christ matters.

Reader's Thoughts:

- April 15 -

A fool is quick-tempered, but a wise person stays calm when insulted.

Proverbs 12:16

Author's Thoughts:

Staying calm when you are insulted requires a pause in your thoughts. This pause gives you a moment to ask for God's guidance. If we are going to be in control of our responses, we must control our temper. If not, we run the risk of being judged by an uncontrolled moment. It is in that moment that a controlled response could be witnessed by a struggling Christian or a nonbeliever. Your actions and reactions can be a witness to the Holy Spirit. Allow the Holy Spirit to fill your thoughts and guide your responses to insults.

Reader's Thoughts:

- April 16 -

Worry weighs a person down; an encouraging word cheers a person up.

Proverbs 12:25

Author's Thoughts:

It wasn't long ago that my response to unpleasant news was immediate worry. My focus was on the problem and not the solution. I am gradually changing how I respond to unpleasant news. I know now that praying instead of worrying is more effective and is clearly a display of my faith in God. My reactions and responses can encourage or discourage others. I pray that your faith continues to be stronger than any challenge God places in your life journey.

Reader's Thoughts:

- April 17 -

Deceit fills hearts that are plotting evil; joy fills hearts that are planning peace!

Proverbs 12:20

Author's Thoughts:

I don't remember a time in my life that I planned evil, but I do remember times when I acted and spoke like evil. For those times, I am sorrowful but forgiven. Joy fills my heart because my heart is filled with appreciation for peace and forgiveness. Peace is a gift that can only come from God, peace that is unexplainable even in challenging times. I praise God for His mercy.

Reader's Thoughts:

- April 18 -

The Lord detests lying lips, but he delights in those who tell the truth.

Proverb 12:22

Author's Thoughts:

I am so thankful that God delights in the truth because mankind seems to prefer a shaded truth. I would prefer the truth even if it is painful. My dear brothers and sisters, please be honest with your partners and/or significant others. Honesty is the foundation for a really good relationship. Honesty motivates longevity in relationships.

Reader's Thoughts:

- April 19 -

The godly give good advice to their friends;
the wicked lead them astray.
Proverbs 12:26

Author's Thoughts:

Most of my family and friends respect my opinions and thoughts. They think that I am a bit wise and give solid advice based on my faith journey and limited knowledge of scripture. I am pleased to have their trust, but it sometimes creates fear in my spirit because the responsibility is tremendous. I am thankful for the opportunity to share my thoughts and thankful for the unwavering support of family and friends.

Reader's Thoughts:

- April 20 -

A wise child accepts a parent's discipline;

a mocker refuses to listen to correction.

Proverbs 13:1

Author's Thoughts:

For some, accepting parental discipline comes automatically, but others put themselves in a position to learn the value of discipline by making mistakes. In small or large ways, we have all mocked discipline, even when we knew that discipline was a result of sin. Developing a relationship with Jesus helps us to understand the beauty of discipline and the value of forgiveness.

Reader's Thoughts:

- April 21 -

Those who control their tongue will have a long life;
opening your mouth can ruin everything.
Proverbs 13:3

Author's Thoughts:

Uncontrolled thoughts that are voiced can make you a slave to sin without Jesus Christ. Living in the spirit with Jesus Christ and in His grace gives you freedom. Our words can be the tool the devil uses to make us sin. Sin loses its power under the shelter of Jesus Christ. Do not let your words cause you to sin. We all were born with a sinful nature. We all have an opportunity to release our sinful ways and move into eternity in Jesus Christ.

Reader's Thoughts:

- April 22 -

Godliness guards the path of the blameless,

but the evil are misled by sin.

Proverbs 13:6

Author's Thoughts:

I cannot count the times that I have been misled by sin in my 59 years of living. I am thankful for Jesus Christ who died on the cross for our sins so that we can all have the opportunity to be made righteous. I really can't say that I have fully given myself to God because I still find myself controlled by sin on occasion. What I can say is that I trust in Jesus and I know He is a forgiving God. I embrace the Holy Spirit and I believe in eternity. I have no fear of death because I am looking forward to opening my eyes to see the face of Jesus.

Reader's Thoughts:

______

______

______

______

______

______

- April 23 -

Some who are poor pretend to be rich;
others who are rich pretend to be poor.
Proverbs 13:7

Author's Thoughts:

The Holy Spirit in us speaks our truth. Your actions as a Christian speak the depth of your faith. Your love for Jesus is reflected in how you treat your neighbor. If we are pretending to love Jesus, your truth will be revealed through your actions. If you are a humble servant, this will be revealed through your impact on mankind.

Reader's Thoughts:

- April 24 -

Pride leads to conflict; those who take advice are wise.

Proverbs 13.10

Author's Thoughts:

I witnessed the life of a prideful person whom I loved dearly for many years. I saw how pride affected his life in negative ways which resulted in many lessons for both of us. I believe that through his pride still arose a beautiful man of God. I believe that God saw the best in him and opened the doors of Heaven on November 22, 2017 at 2:30 PM. I loved that prideful person for 38 years on this earth, and he loved me in spite of my sins. We both will love each other forever and I know he is waiting in Heaven for me. Phillip, I know you are resting in peace.

Reader's Thoughts:

- April 25 -

Wealth from get rich-quick schemes quickly disappears;
wealth from hard work grows over time.
Proverbs 13:11

Author's Thoughts:

It is important to be patient with and for wealth. God determines your wealth. Wealth sometimes can be a teaching tool or a test of your faith. Most of us live abundant lives. God's definition of wealth is different for each of us. There is no need to be envious of your neighbor's wealth. Your wealth just might be your faith in Jesus Christ, which is not always as obvious as monetary wealth. Your wealth might be your children and grandchildren. We should all be thankful for our God-given wealth. What if your wealth was wisdom and you never shared it?

Reader's Thoughts:

- April 26 -

Hope deferred makes the heart sick, but a dream fulfilled is a tree of life.

Proverbs 13:12

Author's Thoughts:

Please pray for those you know who are hopeless. Being hopeless is a gift to the devil because God is hope. How often do we defer hope and accept worry in the place of hope? Staying hopeful requires work on your part. You must feed your mind with positive people, things, and thoughts. You must be a friend to the word of Jesus Christ and a friend of the Holy Spirit. Love is a dear companion to hope.

Reader's Thoughts:

- April 27 -

People who despise advice are asking for trouble;
those who respect a command will succeed.
Proverbs 13:13

Author's Thoughts:

Respecting God's commands and embracing the Holy Spirit leads to a road of righteousness. God's commands are constructive advice. God's commands and Christ-like lifestyle is freedom, and a road to success is defined by the word. Success can come in the form of service. Success doesn't depend on the dollars in your bank account, but rather on the nature of your relationship with Jesus Christ. Success is how well you disciple. Success is embracing the people mankind consider the least of us. Success is loving your neighbor without conditions.

Reader's Thoughts:

- April 28 -

The instruction of the wise is like a life-giving fountain;
those who accept it avoid the snares of death.
Proverbs 13:14

Author's Thoughts:

God-given wisdom is meant to be shared and experienced by others. I am always impressed by people who are wise and don't comprehend their wisdom. People who are wise are humble. Wise people wait before speaking to allow the wisdom of others to be their teacher. I can appreciate people who can identify with wisdom and understand that wisdom is a continuous flow of knowledge and kindness.

Reader's Thoughts:

- April 29 -

Wise people think before they act;

fools don't – and even brag about their foolishness.

Proverbs 13:16

Author's Thoughts:

Applying a thought process before you speak or act decreases foolish reactions and actions. If you don't think before you speak or act, you will end up disappointing yourself, but more importantly, disappointing Jesus. Humble yourself enough to pause and consider the impact of your words and actions on others.

Reader's Thoughts:

- April 30 -

An unreliable messenger stumbles into trouble,
but a reliable messenger brings healing.
Proverbs 13:17

Author's Thoughts:

I believe that if I trust in Jesus, I will never be disgraced. This gives me a foundation for healing and to share God's healing grace. God expects us to be credible in our teaching of His word. God expects us to be examples of how to live out the word. God expects us to admit our faults and ask for forgiveness. In our repentance, we can introduce others to Christ.

Reader's Thoughts:

Reader's Thoughts:

Love Well

~ May ~

Allow the Holy Spirit to fill your thoughts and guide your responses to insults.

- May 1 -

Walk with the wise and become wise; associate with fools and get in trouble.

Proverbs 13:20

Author's Thoughts:

Place your faith in Jesus and He will introduce you to wisdom and to the wise. Understanding that God's power works best in your weaknesses saves you from foolish acts and foolish people. God will give you enough insight to realize when you are walking with unwise people and He will give you the courage to walk away.

Reader's Thoughts:

- May 2 -

Trouble chases sinners, while blessings reward the righteous.

Proverbs 13:21

Author's Thoughts:

If trouble is chasing you, turn your thoughts to Jesus Christ. Believe in your heart that God raised Him from the dead and you will be saved. It is not wise to confuse troubles with trials. Trials are expected in our faith journey. Blessings are revealed through trials.

Reader's Thoughts:

- May 3 -

Those who spare the rod at discipline hate their children.
Those who love their children care enough to discipline them.
Proverbs 13:24

Author's Thoughts:

Discipline can be complicated and difficult without applying the word to your methods and techniques. We all care enough, as parents, to discipline our children, but not all of us understand the value and consequences of proper discipline. I must admit that too often, I didn't discipline my children well because I wasn't always responsible for consequences. Discipline doesn't have a positive impact if you try to block or alter the necessary consequences of the act that lead to discipline. Keep loving your children and holding them accountable for their decisions and actions. Don't forget to pray over your children.

Reader's Thoughts:

- May 4 -

A wise woman builds her home,
but a foolish woman tears it down with her own hands.
Proverbs 14:1

Author's Thoughts:

Women, please do not adapt to low standards in building your home. Your house will remain a house if you do not apply your God given wisdom. It is foolish to think that marriage, or any relationship, is 50/50 because it never was meant to be. Women be loving and patient with your partner and with your children. Please do not tear down your relationships with unwise words; think and pray before you respond to unkind words from others. You can teach others how to treat you in how you apply wisdom.

Reader's Thoughts:

- May 5 -

Those who follow the right path fear the Lord;
those who take the wrong path despise him.
Proverbs 14:2

Author's Thoughts:

Your conscience will always let you know when you are on a wrong path. We must learn to listen to the quiet voice of Jesus Christ. If you are going to be fearful, fear the Lord. He is your protector and He is full of wisdom that He shares with mankind. Your journey in life reflects how you view the Lord, it reflects your degree of commitment to the word, and it reflects how well you love and appreciate the gift of life.

Reader's Thoughts:

- May 6 -

Stay away from fools, for you won't find knowledge on their lips.

Proverbs 14:7

Author's Thoughts:

It is important that our young people learn discernment because they are faced with worldly concerns repeatedly. Good judgement keeps you away from foolish people and things. A fool makes foolish decisions and does foolish things. Oftentimes, a fool's actions are persuasive and convincing to those who do not know Jesus. Relying on Jesus' knowledge and instruction is the perfect way to be unattractive to fools. If someone gives you advice that is harmful, walk away.

Reader's Thoughts:

- May 7 -

The prudent understand where they are going, but fools deceive themselves.

Proverbs 14:8

Author's Thoughts:

There is no better gift than to know that eternity is available to you. Knowing that God's love does no wrong is the key to your journey to eternity. If you love your neighbor as yourself, God's commandments are fulfilled. We all struggle with fulfilling the commandment of love in all that we do and in our reactions to others. The only advice I know is just keep loving well and God will continue to shower you with His love, grace, and mercy.

Reader's Thoughts:

- May 8 -

Fools make fun of guilt, but the godly acknowledge it and seek reconciliation.

Proverbs 14:9

Author's Thoughts:

Guilt is not a sin. Guilt can be a trigger to remind us of God's patience with us. Guilt can be used as a positive motivator for us to reevaluate how we love. Guilt is an opportunity for us to forgive and to be forgiven. Guilt should be temporary because of God's forgiving power. If you feel guilty because you haven't arrived at God's expectations of love, just keep loving.

Reader's Thoughts:

- May 9 -

Each heart knows its own bitterness, and no one else can fully share its joy.

Proverbs 14:10

Author's Thoughts:

Our hearts are conflicted at times. You can acknowledge the bitterness in your heart and share the joys in your heart at the same time. The joy of knowing Jesus Christ is a breakthrough for bitterness. God given joy is perfect and meant to be shared. It is possible to walk through all trials with a joyful spirit. I shoulder my God-given joy every moment of my life and I am proud to voice the source of my joy.

Reader's Thoughts:

- May 10 -

There is a path before each person that seems right, but it ends in death.

Proverbs 14:12

Author's Thoughts:

I urge you to give God a chance to transform your life. You will have no regrets. Eternity will be your comfort and reward. God is love. When I was longer, I feared death. Now that I am older, I embrace the thought of death and I stay motivated to live a life that is pleasing to my soul. I trust God with my soul.

Reader's Thoughts:

- May 11 -

Laughter can conceal a heavy heart,
but when the laughter ends, the grief remains.
Proverbs 14:13

Author's Thoughts:

This is a grieving period for me and my family. We witnessed our beloved Phillip move from this earth into eternity. I will always feel his love because he loved me well. I am thankful to God for giving me an earthly husband that loved me without conditions. How well we loved is inside our three children and will be for generations to come. Yes, laughter can conceal a heavy heart, but joy comes in the morning.

Reader's Thoughts:

- May 12 -

Only simpletons believe everything they're told!
The prudent carefully consider their steps.
Proverbs 14:15

Author's Thoughts:

I don't remember ever believing everything I was told, but I do remember being a simpleton at times. I also remember being simple in my thoughts and ways without any consideration for growth. I still have some simpleton moments, but now I acknowledge and act which results in change. It is necessary for all Christians to apply careful God-like consideration before stepping out into this world. We all need God's guidance to move in our steps with compassion.

Reader's Thoughts:

- May 13 -

Short-tempered people do foolish things, and schemers are hated.

Proverbs 14:17

Author's Thoughts:

God, I pray for patience and understanding. I pray that my responses are measured with a consideration of love. I pray that I don't behave in foolish manners that contradict your commands. Lord help me to open my heart to the needs of your people. Lord please do not allow me to let any action to cause me to hate. Lord thank you for your love and thank you for giving me a hopeful heart. Amen!

Reader's Thoughts:

- May 14 -

The poor are despised even by their neighbors,
while the rich have many "friends."
Proverbs 14:20

Author's Thoughts:

Our communities are separated by class. Class has triggered discomfort towards our fellow mankind. Some measure God's blessings by how big their houses are or how much money they have in their bank accounts. People disregard the blessings of love, service, patience, hope, forgiveness, mercy, and grace. There are some parents who value material things over the love of their children. Jesus who is responsible for love, He wasn't about material wealth. It seems as if we have made material wealth more important than following the word that is inspired by Jesus' life.

Reader's Thoughts:

- May 15 -

It is a sin to belittle one's neighbor, blessed are those who help the poor.

Proverbs 14:21

Author's Thoughts:

There is no room to belittle your neighbor if you love your neighbor as yourself. Love conquers all forms of hate. Love conquers all forms of discrimination. Love conquers all forms of insult. If you love your neighbor, caring for and helping the poor is easy because they are your neighbors. Love well!

Reader's Thoughts:

- May 16 -

If you plan to do evil, you will be lost; if you plan to do good, you will receive unfailing love and faithfulness.

Proverbs 14:22

Author's Thoughts:

It takes an abundance of energy and thoughts to do evil. Doing evil removes you from the safety of Jesus Christ. God's love and faithfulness is a beautiful reflection of approval. Good and evil can't share the same space in your heart. You either chase good or chase evil. Chasing good is life everlasting; chasing evil is a sure way of missing out on longevity.

Reader's Thoughts:

- May 17 -

People with understanding control their anger;
a hot temper shows great foolishness.
Proverbs 14:29

Author's Thoughts:

I must admit that God blessed me with the power of control for most situations. My responses are usually measured, but when they are not measured, I feel the uncomfortable circumstances. I don't ever remember being hot tempered, but I do remember being inconsiderate in my so-called restrained comments and responses to others' comments. I continue to pray for control and for positive unhurried responses. Be thankful for God's forgiveness.

Reader's Thoughts:

- May 18 -

A peaceful heart leads to a healthy body; jealousy is like cancer in the bones.

Proverbs 14:30

Author's Thoughts:

Jealousy is such a bad trait. Jealousy can quickly ruin a relationship. Jealousy is a huge sign of distrust. Jealousy spreads throughout our thoughts and actions and creates destruction. Jealousy doesn't appreciate others' blessings. Jealousy destroys marriages and families. Jealousy promotes insecurities. Jealousy separates Christians. Jealousy hinders peace. Jealousy is not of God.

Reader's Thoughts:

Those who oppress the poor insult their Maker, but helping the poor honors him.

Proverbs 14:31

Author's Thoughts:

Our hearts should favor the poor. We can honor Jesus Christ by honoring the least of His people. God is pleased when we help others with blessings from God. It is not easy to overlook the poor in our society because the needs of the poor are evident. The poor need what you need, which is love, and compassion from our fellow mankind. It is through loving and helping hands that the poor can experience Jesus Christ. Oppressing the poor is easy; loving the poor is expressing your belief and faith in Jesus Christ.

Reader's Thoughts:

- May 20 -

Wisdom is enshrjned in an understanding heart;

wisdom is not found among fools.

Proverbs 14:33

Author's Thoughts:

I pray that my children have understanding and loving hearts so that generations to come will be affected by their hearts. I would like to think that my children's father and I gifted them with hearts that are of hope, love, and kindness. Wisdom is a perfect gift for our children to experience by seeing how we as parents accept and live out God-given wisdom.

Reader's Thoughts:

- May 21 -

Godliness makes a nation great, but sin is a disgrace to any people.

Proverbs 14:34

Author's Thoughts:

Fake godliness is no match for true "godliness". Our nation will only be great when its leaders are men and women of faith. Leaders exercising fake godliness will be disgraced. God sees all and knows all. Great nations are built on love for all of mankind.

Great nations do not leave the poor behind. Great nations understand that we all matter. Humble leaders lead great nations.

Reader's Thoughts:

- May 22 -

A gentle answer deflects anger, but harsh words make tempers flare.

Proverbs 15:1

Author's Thoughts:

A quiet and gentle spirit can calm anger. If you approach anger with anger the devil will control the outcome. If you bring calm to a situation with anger already at the table, you can control your actions and words and might encourage calmness around the table. Peaceful words and actions bring stability to life and control to your actions.

Reader's Thoughts:

- May 23 -

The tongue of the wise makes knowledge appealing,
but the mouth of a fool belches out foolishness.
Proverbs 15:2

Author's Thoughts:

Be patient and trust God's faithfulness. A wise tongue reflects a willingness to compromise and a desire to be silent when necessary. Wisdom sometimes is better expressed in silence. It is important to sometimes listen to the words of the foolish to better understand their hearts. It is never good to follow the advice of a foolish person. God's wisdom will help you discern and identify fools.

Reader's Thoughts:

- May 24 -

The Lord is watching everywhere,
keeping his eye on both the evil and the good.
Proverbs 15:3

Author's Thoughts:

I am pleased that God's hears all and sees all. Even knowing that God is all-knowing, I still sin, and He still graces me with His love, mercy, and forgiveness. There is no one greater than God. There is no one fairer than God. There is no one more forgiving than God. There is no one more hopeful than God. There is no one more forgiving than God. There is no one more patient than God. I accept grace and mercy from none other than God. I am thankful that God's eyes are on evil because He is my protector.

Reader's Thoughts:

- May 25 -

Gentle words are a tree of life; a deceitful tongue crushes the spirit.

Proverbs 15:4

Author's Thoughts:

Man-o-man, I can't count the times that my words offended people that I love. Man-o-man, I can't count the times that God forgave me, turned me around, and made me clean again. God can be trusted to do all that He said He would do. When your heart is crushed by someone with a deceitful tongue, just pray for them and ask for God's mercy on the situation and the people involved. God can change the hearts of foolish and evil people. Your prayers are heard and acted on by Jesus Christ.

Reader's Thoughts:

- May 26 -

The lips of the wise give good advice; the heart of a fool has none to give.

Proverbs 15:7

Author's Thoughts:

If we are not watchful, we can be fooled by foolish people with foolish advice. It is important that we get to know the hearts and faith of those who we seek out for advice. Goodness comes from the mouths of the wise. Conflict results from foolish advice. Use good judgement when you are giving advice or receiving advice. Always remember that Jesus' wisdom is perfect, and don't forget to consult with Him.

Reader's Thoughts:

- May 27 -

Mockers hate to be corrected, so they stay away from the wise.

Proverbs 15:12

Author's Thoughts:

Mockers tend to lack self-confidence. It is possible for mockers to learn from the wise, but at an observant distance. There is no better lesson than an experienced lesson. We should never give up on mockers; God loves mockers.

Reader's Thoughts:

- May 28 -

A glad heart makes a happy face; a broken heart crushes the spirit.

Proverbs 15:13

Author's Thoughts:

We should pursue happy. Happiness is such a special gift. Happiness leads to joy, and joy leads to peace. It is wonderful when we can bring happy to a relationship instead of putting pressure on others to be the source of our happiness. A broken heart can crush the spirit of people we love. Sometimes we allow sadness to guide us down an unhappy path. Sadness can turn into joy in your next breath.

Reader's Thoughts:

- May 29 -

A wise person is hungry for knowledge, while the fool feeds on trash.

Proverbs 15:14

Author's Thoughts:

Trash can be attractive if we forget the value of wisdom. It is a blessing when we feed on wisdom and not on dirt. I am hungry for the word. A 365-day read opened my heart to the Old Testament and made my heart even hungrier for the New Testament. I am so appreciative for the Bible, it is a source of wisdom.

Reader's Thoughts:

- May 30 -

Better to have little, with fear for the Lord,

than to have great treasure and inner turmoil.

Proverbs 15:16

Author's Thoughts:

Gone are the days and nights of inner conflict. I now experience an intimate relationship with Jesus Christ. My greatest treasure is God's love for me. I am very thankful for the peace that accompanies hope and faith. I trust God's faithfulness. Inner conflict creates doubt and doubt restricts your faith. I cannot put into words how free I felt when I stopped worrying about things that hadn't happened. I discovered a deeper trust in God.

Reader's Thoughts:

- May 31 -

A bowl of vegetables with someone you love is better
than steak with someone you hate.
Proverbs 15:17

Author's Thoughts:

Love is the foundation of my heart. I pray often that God gives my heart what it needs to love well and to love without conditions. It is a wonderful feeling when you are on the receiving end of love, but it is really good when you share love. Love makes vegetables appealing.

Reader's Thoughts:

- June -

Arrogance and pride will lead to destruction even if the journey to destruction seems fruitful at times.

- June 1 -

A lazy person's way is blocked with briers,
but the path of the upright is an open highway.
Proverbs 15:19

Author's Thoughts:

Your life can be an open highway on a journey to embrace the love of Jesus Christ. You can do your journey on a narrow one-way street or an open highway with numerous lanes. That narrow way of life is blocked with many barriers. The open highway allows you to go around the barriers. Why restrict your faith, let it explore God's love on an open highway to eternity.

Reader's Thoughts:

- June 2 -

Everyone enjoys a fitting reply;
it is wonderful to say the right thing at the right time.
Proverbs 15:23

Author's Thoughts:

At times it is difficult to know what a fitting reply is. Each set of circumstances require an appropriate thought process. It is wise to consider your thoughts before you speak. You might not always say the right words at the right time, but careful consideration will lessen your opportunity to say unfortunate words. We all can appreciate careful and thoughtful advice.

Reader's Thoughts:

- June 3 -

Greed brings grief to the whole family, but those who hate bribes will live.

Proverbs 15:27

Author's Thoughts:

Making an honest dollar is music to your soul. Greed contradicts an appreciation for a humble and honest lifestyle. Greed will ultimately destroy your soul and can destroy your family. It is important to be content in the positions that God places you in. All of us are not made up to be monetarily wealthy, but we are gifted with the willpower to overcome trials.

Reader's Thoughts:

- June 4 -

A cheerful look brings joy to the heart; good news makes for good health.

Proverbs 15:30

Author's Thoughts:

Smile, you can change how others view the world with a smile. A smile is a display of joy. Joy shows so much grace. Joy in you motivates change in others. My health improved tremendously when I began to control my emotions and control how I responded to unpleasant news. Good beliefs and a positive perspective makes for good health.

Reader's Thoughts:

- June 5 -

If you listen to constructive criticism, you will be at home among the wise.

Proverbs 15:31

Author's Thoughts:

Appreciating constructive criticism was a process for me. I can appreciate constructive criticism from sensible people, but I can also dismiss criticism that is without wisdom My spiritual growth has been enhanced by the loving advice and teachings of people of God. My mother, Mildred Crook, is an excellent example of someone who applies constructive criticism to most situations and circumstances. I can always depend on her to be honest and straight forward in her responses. I am so thankful to be blessed with a mother who is faithful. She is blessed with discernment.

Reader's Thoughts:

- June 6 -

Fear of the Lord teaches wisdom; humility precedes honor.

Proverbs 15:33

Author's Thoughts:

Honor is valuable with humility. I always feel God's presence when my heart is filled with modesty. Love flows in me through humble acts of kindness. I fear God because I love and respect His ways. I have a tremendous appreciation for God because He gave His only son, Jesus, to die on the cross for our sins. So thankful!

Reader's Thoughts:

- June 7 -

We can make out own plans, but the Lord gives the right answer.

Proverbs 16:1

Author's Thoughts:

God's plans are always perfect. In order for us to believe that His plans are perfect we must be patient with His plans and we must trust His ways. I can remember many times when my faith was weak and I simply didn't think God even had plans for my life. I now know that I must be comfortable when God makes adjustments to my plans or redirects my plans. I must have the faith that God's plans for me are far better than any plans I could ever make for myself.

Reader's Thoughts:

- June 8 -

People may be pure in their own eyes, but the Lord examines their motives.

Proverb 16:2

Author's Thoughts:

Always remember that God knows and sees all things even your thoughts and motives. I can't remember a time when I thought I was completely pure in my eyes, but I am hopeful that God sees purity in me. I welcome God's examination of my heart because it encourages me to be hopeful and faithful. The more I love God, the more growth I experience.

Reader's Thoughts:

- June 9 -

Unfailing love and faithfulness make atonement for sins.

By fearing the Lord, people avoid evil.

Proverbs 16:6

Author's Thoughts:

I can never be sure that Phillip, my husband of 26 years, received my love as unfailing, but I am sure that I loved him well. I am sure that he received my forgiveness and love because I loved him deeply and I forgave him for all of his faults that had a negative influence on our marriage. I know in my heart that he forgave me for my faults.

Your faithful service and forgiving love honors God.

Reader's Thoughts:

- June 10 -

When people's lives please the Lord,
even their enemies are at peace with them.
Proverbs 16:7

Author's Thoughts:

Living pure and blameless is what God expects of us. God also knows that we are sinners which is why I strongly believe that He is all powerful, all loving, and all forgiving. As we grow in the knowledge and understanding of Jesus' ways, our lives should move closer to pure and blameless. We learn to obey God with the deepest of reverence.

Reader's Thoughts:

- June 11 -

Better to have little, with godliness, than to be rich and dishonest.

Proverbs 16:8

Author's Thoughts:

It is better to be rich in humility than rich in material things. It is better to take the humble position of a servant than to be dishonest. God purchased our freedom with the blood of His son, not with money or material riches. Having nominal material riches keeps you hopeful in the unseen. Living a life in goodness pleases God.

Reader's Thoughts:

- June 12 -

The Lord demands accurate scales and balances;

he sets the standards for fairness.

Proverbs 16:11

Author's Thoughts:

Glory be to God for his fairness of standards. Glory be to God for His grace and mercy. Glory be to God for His service to others. Glory be to God for His patience and understanding. Glory be to God for His son, Jesus Christ. Glory be to God that we do not have to live in a world without hope. Glory be to God for a sense of shame. Glory be to God for joy. Amen.

Reader's Thoughts:

- June 13 -

The king is pleased with words from righteous lips;
he loves those who speak honestly.
Proverbs 16:13

Author's Thoughts:

To speak from righteous lips to one another is much like a song of praise to God's ears We speak from righteous lips when speak of things pertaining to God's kingdom tc each other. We reflect the glory of our King Jesus when our speech is seasoned with grace humility, sincerity, and genuine love. In doing so, we literally manifest His divine natur toward each other, and toward the world around us. To speak deceitfully, pridefully maliciously, or rudely, is a betrayal and denial of our relationship with our amazing King.

Reader's Thoughts:

- June 14 -

How much better to get wisdom than gold, and good judgment than silver!

Proverbs 16:16

Author's Thoughts:

I actually pray for wisdom and good judgment because I can be quick to respond without proper thought and preparation. Wisdom and good judgment, for me, is a continual journey. God has really blessed me with the confidence to know that He will provide me with the proper wisdom and good judgment in all situations. If I speak without thinking or listening to God's gentle voice, that is not God's fault. Reflecting on God before responding is a personal challenge.

Reader's Thoughts:

- June 15 -

Pride goes before destruction, and haughtiness before a fall.

Proverbs 16:18

Author's Thoughts:

We should all have been concerned about the state of America in 2017. Many of us, including me, at times, were more concerned with party lines than with godliness and dignity. Arrogance and pride will lead to destruction even if the journey to destruction seems fruitful at times. We have cause to be hopeful because Jesus Christ came into this world to save sinners, even the worst of sinners. Hold strong in your faith and don't let power or money cause you to waiver. Pray for our leaders!

Reader's Thoughts:

- June 16 -

Better to live humbly with the poor than to share plunder with the proud.

Proverbs 16:19

Author's Thoughts:

Traits of pride, vanity, arrogance, and self-importance have always made me uncomfortable. When one or more of these traits enter my spirit, I immediately Acknowledge them and start the journey of releasing those behaviors from my heart. It is difficult to understand the hearts and minds of the poor if we are prideful. Helping the poor and less fortunate requires an unjudging and loving heart. It is mandatory that all living souls know that they matter and that they are loved.

Reader's Thoughts:

- June 17 -

Those who listen to instruction will prosper; those who trust the Lord will be joyful.

Proverbs 16:20

Author's Thoughts:

Trusting the Lord requires a persistent relationship with Him. Your faith must be nourished with the word and with positive Christ-like people feeding you with meaningful discussions. Listen to the advice of the wise and trust your relationship with Christ Jesus.

Reader's Thoughts:

- June 18 -

The wise are known for their understanding, and pleasant words are persuasive.

Proverbs 16:21

Author's Thoughts:

Wisdom from God can't be concealed. A wise person of God is filled with love and faith that comes from Jesus Christ. A wise person of God can identify those whose teachings are contrary to God's teachings. A wise person's advice is genuine and is consistent with good. A wise person's words are acceptable to God and compelling, although not always agreeable to others.

Reader's Thoughts:

- June 19 -

Discretion is a life-giving fountain to those who possess it,

but discipline is wasted on fools.

Proverbs 16:22

Author's Thoughts:

Discretion is a valuable gift and it requires a continuous thought process before speaking. Discretion is necessary to avoid causing offense to others in our words and actions. It is more important, for me, to be mindful of trustful relationships that require special emotional discretion. A Christ-like person chooses good judgement and is protective of private information.

Reader's Thoughts:

From a wise mind comes wise speech; the words of the wise are persuasive.

Proverbs 16:23

Author's Thoughts:

If God blessed you with wisdom you must respect that blessing enough to use your words wisely. When you develop a Christ-like reputation for wisdom, others depend on your advice. Please be mindful as you teach others through your words and actions. Genuine faith is revealed through how you live your life journey. "The words of the wise are persuasive" is such an insightful statement.

Reader's Thoughts:

- June 21 -

Kind words are like honey-sweet to the soul and healthy for the body.

Proverbs 16:24

Author's Thoughts:

We all love kind and considerate words and people. If you are filled with hope and love, your words will be consistent. It is only by God's grace that we are saved, and it is God's grace that gives us loving and kind spirits. We are obligated to share God's gifts with others. If kind words are like honey, why not spread the honey around to motivate healthy souls?

Reader's Thoughts:

- June 22 -

A troublemaker plants seeds of strife; gossip separates the best of friends.

Proverbs 16:28

Author's Thoughts:

Gossip has always made me uncomfortable. Age taught me to walk away from gossip and assess the gossipers. If you find yourself with a group of people who gossip about someone as soon as that person left the conversation, you can exit the conversation in disagreement. Without a judgmental attitude, let them know that gossip makes you uncomfortable. Why spend time talking about details that may not be true? God please protect us from gossip and reprimand our hearts when we gossip.

Reader's Thoughts:

- June 23 -

Violent people mislead their companions, leading them down a harmful path.

Proverbs 16:29

Author's Thoughts:

Wisdom and good judgment of character are precious favors. It is challenging to see someone you love with poor judgement being misled by others. It seems the more you try to "wise them up," the more they allow themselves to be misled. Sometimes the path is harmful for your loved one and others affected by that path. It is important to stay true to the word and continue to be examples of hope. We can't give up because God is faithful.

Reader's Thoughts:

- June 24 -

With narrowed eyes, people plot evil; with a smirk, they plan their mischief.

Proverbs 16:30

Author's Thoughts:

Evil has no power against the armor of Jesus Christ. Yes, people do plan evil and mischief against each other, and sometimes Christians against Christians. The response to evil is prayer and an intimate relationship with Jesus. Evil can rule in your life without God. Be on guard for evil doers so that you will have a proper response.

Reader's Thoughts:

- June 25 -

Gray hair is a crown of glory; it is gained by living a godly life.

Proverbs 16:31

Author's Thoughts:

My entire head only grows gray hair now. I simply learned to embrace gray hair and see it as a sign of respect for a life well lived. Gray hair can be associated with wisdom or it can only be associated with old age. I prefer wisdom and living a godly life. Guess I will wear my "crown of glory" with pride. When God saves you from a life altering illness, gray hair is respected. So thankful for the gift of life.

Reader's Thoughts:

- June 26 -

Better to be patient than powerful;
better to have self-control than to conquer a city.
Proverbs 16:32

Author's Thoughts:

When God saved us through His kindness we were given the power to exercise self-control, then we became worthy of respect. We were saved by God who is filled with love and kindness. We can live through and in God's love and kindness or we can give it back in our actions. It is how we live that measures our faithful commitment to Jesus Christ.

Reader's Thoughts:

- June 27 -

We may throw the dice, but the Lord determines how they fall.

Proverbs 16:33

Author's Thoughts:

I am so thankful that God determines our steps and He can redirect our steps in each moment. You can be a slave to lust and pleasures or a slave for God. You can be foolish and dishonest, or a slave for God. You can only meet your needs or meet the needs of others as well. You can be filled with love and patience or you can hate without patience. You can have a considerate heart or you can be inconsiderate. You can love goodness or not appreciate goodness. You can live in joy or live unhappy. You can be hopeful or hopeless. You can forgive or not experience forgiveness. You can love or hate. You can live a peaceful life or cause confusion. We all have choices!

Reader's Thoughts:

- June 28 -

Better a dry crust eaten in peace than a house filled with feasting and conflict.

Proverbs 17:1

Author's Thoughts:

Be content with God's definition of enough and you will experience His grace, mercy, and peace. Remember that your faithful service is your offering to God. Remove conflict from your life by listening to the Holy Spirit. The Holy Spirit will speak to you and gently guide you away from sin, but you must be willing.

Reader's Thoughts:

- June 29 -

Fire tests the purity of silver and gold, but the Lord tests the heart.

Proverbs 17:3

Author's Thoughts:

Sometimes I would like to pause and not let God in my heart until I have cleaned it out. In those times, I need the Holy Spirit to come into my heart and to change my heart. We can't do anything good without God. Invite Him into your heart, ask for forgiveness, repent, and move in the Holy Spirit. You can experience the joy that doesn't depend on your circumstances because it is rooted in Christ Jesus.

Reader's Thoughts:

- June 30 -

Wrongdoers eagerly listen to gossip; liars pay close attention to slander.

Proverbs 17:4

Author's Thoughts:

Live a life that looks down on gossip. Be kind, fair, loving, patient, and stay hopeful. These characteristics are an enemy to gossip. When others see you in a conversation they should be motivated not to gossip. Open their minds to a sense of shame. Live so that others will want to know your favor. You live in a world with Jesus. You live in a world with hope.

Reader's Thoughts:

Reader's Thoughts:

Reprimands from God should change our souls.

- July 1 -

Those who mock the poor insult their Maker;
those who rejoice at the misfortune of others will be punished.
Proverbs 17:5

Author's Thoughts:

I am offended when I hear or see someone mistreating God's people especially those less fortunate. It is probably, in part, because my family was less fortunate and to many, I am less fortunate. Whatever the reasons are, I am offended when Christians are so closed-minded that they fail to see Jesus in those in need. It is only by God's grace that one can consider themselves fortunate and live a life of abundance. Remember that those in need and those that we tend to look down on are children of God, and I dare to say that they consider themselves fortunate.

Reader's Thoughts:

- July 2 -

A single rebuke does more for a person of understanding
than a hundred lashes on the back of a fool.
Proverbs 17:10

Author's Thoughts:

Paying attention and acknowledging God's reprimands can be a humbling experience. If God disapproves of your actions, He will steer your heart and reprimand you when necessary. Reprimands are food to the souls of Christians. Reprimands from God should change our souls. Christians, stop being foolish, listen to God's teachings and respond to His rebukes with a deeper understanding of His ways.

Reader's Thoughts:

- July 3 -

If you repay good with evil, evil will never leave your house.

Proverbs 17:13

Author's Thoughts:

If you respond to evil with good, your foundation in Christ will be firm. There are lots of evil repayments going on in our households. The divorce rate is an indicator of partners repaying evil with evil and sometimes evil is a response to good. Christians are to forgive, we do not hold onto pain that gave support to an evil foundation in our hearts. Love really does cover an abundance of sins.

Reader's Thoughts:

- July 4 -

It is senseless to pay tuition to educate a fool, since he has no heart for learning.

Proverbs 17:16

Author's Thoughts:

How many of us parents sent a foolish child off to college and foolishly expected them to do well? God protects fools, both parent and child. Amen!

Reader's Thoughts:

- July 5 -

It is painful to be the parent of a fool; there is no joy for the father of a rebel.

Proverbs 17:21

Author's Thoughts:

Rebels are not always rebels. Fools are not always fools. Pain doesn't last forever. Disappointment is temporary. Joy comes in Jesus Christ. Stay strong in your faith and live pure and humble lives. You can teach your foolish children about the love of Christ in how you live out your life journey. Making foolish decisions can provide a path to change. I must admit, I still sometimes make foolish decisions that impact others in negative ways. God is such a forgiving God.

Reader's Thoughts:

- July 6 -

A cheerful heart is good medicine, but a broken spirit saps a person's strength.

Proverbs 17:22

Author's Thoughts:

A broken spirit is a sign of a hopeless heart. God paid for our freedom with the blood of Jesus Christ. In that blood, our sins were forgiven. Let your life bring honor to Jesus Christ for dying on the cross for our sins. Pay attention to and cultivate your heart so that your spirit is protected. Let your joy be rooted in Jesus Christ.

Reader's Thoughts:

- July 7 -

Foolish children bring grief to their father
and bitterness to the one who gave them birth.
Proverbs 17:25

Author's Thoughts:

We must be patient with the foolish generations of young people because we are responsible for some of their foolishness. Some of us as parents and protectors failed to focus on the power of God while caring for our children, instead, we focused on the power of money. The majority of millennials seem to focus on how to acquire meaningless material things instead of how to protect their souls. As teachers and protectors, it is never too late to introduce your children and others to the faith of Jesus Christ. It is never too late to be a reflection of Jesus in how you live in your faith.

Reader's Thoughts:

- July 8 -

A truly wise person uses few words;

a person with understanding is even-tempered.

Proverbs 17:27

Author's Thoughts:

Silence is a valuable tool to use to communicate. A silent response allows others to speak and to hear themselves speak. Silence is sometimes a gentle and respectful way of communicating disagreement in other's thoughts. Wisdom can flow through silence.

Reader's Thoughts:

- July 9 -

Even fools are thought wise when they keep silent;
with their mouths shut, they seem intelligent.
Proverbs 17:28

Author's Thoughts:

Just because fools are silent doesn't mean that their hearts are not open to humble wisdom. Silent fools are listening to the communicators and will react to what is said through actions. Silent fools can identify evil ways and evil words. Silent fools love to listen to people with humble attitudes and tender hearts. Wisdom is available to all of foolish mankind.

Reader's Thoughts:

- July 10 -

Fools have no interest in understanding; they only want to air their own opinions.

Proverbs 18:2

Author's Thoughts:

This verse touched my soul because determining when to air my opinion is sometimes a struggle for me, but I am a much better listener than I used to be. I am always interested in understanding, but I am not always patient enough to listen so that understanding is possible. I pray that we all listen to God's humble spirit in Jesus Christ.

Reader's Thoughts:

- July 11 -

Wise words are like deep waters;

wisdom flows from the wise like a bubbling brook.

Proverbs 18:4

Author's Thoughts:

Wise people have always intrigued me. I have always been drawn to age and insight. I have deep respect for people who are wise and speak with astuteness but are so humble that they don't realize the depth of their knowledge. I trust wise and respectful people with proven track records.

Reader's Thoughts:

- July 12 -

It is not right to acquit the guilty or deny justice to the innocent.

Proverbs 18:5

Author's Thoughts:

The innocent and poor in our society seem to be denied justice too often by enforcers who are unreasonable and who can't extend mercy when warranted. Justice can be purchased with money, but eternity was purchased by the blood of Jesus and can't be purchased with your bank account. We all should have an opportunity for real justice without a price tag.

Reader's Thoughts:

- July 13 -

Rumors are dainty morsels that sink deep into one's heart.

Proverbs 18:8

Author's Thoughts:

If the message is rumored, it shouldn't be repeated. It takes one person to put an end to a rumor. Give the rumor credit for being an untruth and this should motivate you not to repeat an untruth that will only create hurt. An apology for repeating a rumor is good for the person who is the source of the rumor. Rumors can result in a long period of rebuilding trust.

Reader's Thoughts:

- July 14 -

The name of the Lord is a strong fortress; the godly run to him and are safe.

Proverbs 18:10

Author's Thoughts:

You are safe with the Lord.

You can trust the Lord.

You are strong in the Lord.

You can receive the Lord's grace and mercy.

You are protected in the Lord.

Your salvation comes through the Lord.

Keep running to the Lord, He is patient and hopeful.

Reader's Thoughts:

- July 15 -

The first to speak in court sounds right- until the cross-examination begins.

Proverbs 18:17

Author's Thoughts:

This verse reminds me of Elihu in the Book of Job. Elihu was the last and the youngest who provided Job with advice. The truth from young or old will stand the test of time. Elihu's advice impacted Job in profound ways. My son Elihu continues to impact my life in profound ways. Blessings provide room in our hearts to be thankful in all circumstances.

Reader's Thoughts:

- July 16 -

Wise words satisfy like a good meal; the right words bring satisfaction.

Proverbs 18:20

Author's Thoughts:

Wise words can comfort a broken heart. Wise words accompanied by strong faith can introduce Jesus to unbelievers. Our words and actions either embody Jesus or the devil. It is necessary for us to examine our thoughts before offering advice. Allow God to use you to impact others in profound ways. A humble attitude is immeasurable.

Reader's Thoughts:

- July 17 -

The man who finds a wife finds a treasure, and he receives favor from the Lord.

Proverbs 18:22

Author's Thoughts:

I can honestly say that I really tussled with being a treasure to my husband until I developed an intimate relationship with God. I am sure Phillip thought I was a treasure even in my weakest moments. I am sure Phillip received favor from God because of some of my actions as a wife and I am sure I received favor because of Phillip's actions. I pray for the covenant of marriage and I pray that couples focus on hope, love, mercy, grace, and forgiveness. I now know that Phillip was my treasure. I miss his love and kindness.

Reader's Thoughts:

- July 18 -

The poor plead for mercy; the rich answer with insults.

Proverbs 18:23

Author's Thoughts:

The poor can easily be misled by the rich. The poor can easily be abused by the rich. The poor can easily be insulted by the rich. The poor can easily be looked down upon by the rich. The poor can easily be used by the rich. The rich should realize that the weakness of the poor can be turned into strength. We all, rich or poor, are given an opportunity to speak to others through our faith and we are all made right with God through our faith in Jesus Christ.

Reader's Thoughts:

- July 19 -

There are "friends" who destroy each other,
but a real friend sticks closer than a brother.
Proverbs 18:24

Author's Thoughts:

God has blessed me with several really loyal friends; women of God who I trust and believe in their love. Women of this world, please develop relationships with like-minded women who uplift your soul and can pray for you and your family. Loyal friends are true gifts from God. Trust in your friends who understand that love binds us together in perfect harmony. To all of my trusted friends, thanks for your love and support.

Reader's Thoughts:

- July 20 -

Better to be poor and honest than to be dishonest and a fool.

Proverbs 19:1

Author's Thoughts:

I have been poor and foolish at times. I learned to be honest with my heart and have no shame in being honest about my prior and present sin. I am no longer a fool and I shy away from dishonesty at all times. I am thankful that God protects me even when I am foolish, and that He forgives my dishonest thoughts and ways. Integrity is of utmost importance to my being. God, please forgive me when I fall short of your desires for my heart.

Reader's Thoughts:

- July 21 -

Enthusiasm without knowledge is no good; haste makes mistakes.

Proverbs 19:2

Author's Thoughts:

Is it even possible to count the times that mistakes were made in haste and without talking with God? The eagerness in making a rush decision can make for a temporary fix that doesn't withstand the necessary test. Haste does make for mistakes, but faith is more powerful than the mistakes. Keep feeding your soul with good knowledge and your mistakes will be reduced.

Reader's Thoughts:

- July 22 -

People ruin their lives by their own foolishness and then are angry at the Lord.

Proverbs 19:3

Author's Thoughts:

I can say with confidence that my foolishness has never resulted in me being angry with God. I can't remember a time that my personal trials took me down a path that caused me to be angry with God. My trials have taken me to my knees as a place to cry out to the Lord. My trials have affected my emotions in ways that caused me to question God, but never angry. My faith journey is at a place where I question God less and rely on His amazing strength.

Reader's Thoughts:

- July 23 -

Wealth makes many "friends;" poverty drives them all away.

Proverbs 19:4

Author's Thoughts:

Some of us are wealthy in spirit not in material things and money. I can't remember a time when the spirit of love and self-discipline drove people away from me. However, I can remember times when being poor drove people away. If we chose to live Holy among believers and nonbelievers, we are doing God's will and not the will of the people. Trying to do the will of mankind takes us away from God's will.

Reader's Thoughts:

- July 24 -

To acquire wisdom is to love oneself;
people who cherish understanding will prosper.
Proverbs 19:8

Author's Thoughts:

Your weakness can be turned into your most valuable strengths. If your weakness is not understanding the Bible, get to know this wonderful book that is inspired by God. Stop saying what you don't understand and be motivated by knowledge. The scripture between the cover of the Bible teaches us to be faithful and to do good work. Being under a good and gentle instructor of the word is immeasurable, but embracing the word in our personal devotion is Holy.

Reader's Thoughts:

- July 25 -

Sensible people control their temper; they earn respect by overlooking wrongs.

Proverbs 19:11

Author's Thoughts:

Overlooking wrongs doesn't mean that you forget the wrong, it means that you forgive the wrong. Forgiving is a measure of control and a measure of accepting Jesus. God expects us to live in the spirit of love. Love motivates forgiveness. Forgiveness pleases God and reveals our love for Jesus. Forgiveness requires self-control and self-discipline.

Reader's Thoughts:

- July 26 -

A foolish child is a calamity to a father;

a quarrelsome wife is as annoying as constant dripping.

Proverbs 19:13

Author's Thoughts:

A foolish child needs parents whose faith is evident and genuine. A foolish child needs to be introduced to Jesus Christ. A foolish child needs to feel unconditional love. A foolish child needs to see Jesus in their parents. A quarrelsome wife needs to see Jesus in her husband. A quarrelsome wife needs to be loved and respected. A quarrelsome wife needs gentle Christ-like instructions and guidance. We all need Jesus.

Reader's Thoughts:

- July 27 -

Fathers can give their sons an inheritance of houses and wealth,
but only the Lord can give an understanding wife.

Proverbs 19:14

Author's Thoughts:

An understanding and loving wife is worthy of respect and worthy of consistent love. Understanding women are gentle and caring. Those who would like to be married should ask God for the kind of spouse worthy of their love. It is not wise to leave God out of your decision-making process when selecting a spouse. Be patient in the process.

Reader's Thoughts:

- July 28 -

Keep the commandments and keep your life; despising them leads to death.

Proverbs 19:16

Author's Thoughts:

God made our hearts and souls prepared to keep His commandments. If you love God with all your might, and love your neighbors as you love yourself, you will have eternal life. Disregarding and despising the commandments shows a disrespect for God's sacrifice of His only son to save us from sin. Disregard for the commandments leads you with no protection from the devil.

Reader's Thoughts:

- July 29 -

If you help the poor, you are lending to the Lord-and he will repay you!

Proverbs 19:17

Author's Thoughts:

My efforts to help the less fortunate have been rewarded in endless ways. I don't help expecting anything in return; I help because my heart leads me to be of service. My desire is to be that one person that a soul needs to feel that they matter. I do not want to walk by Jesus without acknowledging His love and hope. I am of the opinion that Jesus shows up in the needy and He waits for the fortunate to respond in love and with kindness. You matter!

Reader's Thoughts:

- July 30 -

Hot-tempered people must pay the penalty.
If you rescue them once, you will have to do it again.
Proverbs 19:19

Author's Thoughts:

It has been such a challenge over the years to control my facial expressions during meetings and in conversations with coworkers. My expressions speak for me, even when I don't say a word, and when I do not want to voice my opinions. My lack of outward control has created many uncomfortable challenges for me, but I continue to pray through them. Hope is part of my soul, so I am confident that I will overcome.

Reader's Thoughts:

- July 31 -

Get all the advice and instruction you can, so you will be wise the rest of your life.

Proverbs 19:20

Author's Thoughts:

It is important that we pay attention to and listen to the wise people God places on our paths. God often speaks wisdom through others. Wisdom is a beautiful journey with moment by moment impactful lessons. Consider yourself wise when you have the discernment to recognize a lesson from the wise and listen to the wise. The Book of Proverbs is an excellent platform for understanding the value of wisdom.

Reader's Thoughts:

August

We must be equipped with judgment wrapped in wisdom because the devil never stops trying to confuse us.

- August 1 -

You can make many plans, but the Lord's purpose will prevail.

Proverbs 19:21

Author's Thoughts:

When we were raising our three children, I always had to have a plan for days and events. Phillip chose to walk in moments without plans. Phillip was better at leaving space in his time for God to reveal His purpose for each moment. Now that our children are grown and they taught me that God's plans will prevail, I leave room for God. It's funny how we learn to appreciate each other outside of the moment.

Reader's Thoughts:

- August 2 -

Loyalty makes a person attractive. It is better to be poor than dishonest.

Proverbs 19:22

Author's Thoughts:

Loyalty must be earned. No one should be asked to be loyal to a dishonest person whether that person is rich or poor. Loyalty is to be honored and respected with no opportunity for your loyalty to be abused. I am a very loyal person, but I am also very protective of loyalty.

Reader's Thoughts:

- August 3 -

Fear of the Lord leads to life, bringing security and protection from harm.

Proverbs 19:23

Author's Thoughts:

It is healthy and freeing to fear the Lord. Fear of the Lord doesn't always prevent sin, but it is the best deterrence ever. The fact that Jesus died on the cross for our sin should promote loyalty to love, hope, intolerance for sin, grace, mercy, forgiveness, patience, and understanding. Those wonderful traits are Christ-like and sin-killers. Christ-like actions are security and protection against sin.

Reader's Thoughts:

- August 4 -

Lazy people take food in their hand but don't even lift it to their mouth.

Proverbs 19:24

Author's Thoughts:

Lazy people tend to have no follow up. Their intentions are good, but they lack motivation. Success passes them by because it requires dedication and hard work. Faith is sometimes challenging because it requires nourishment. Lazy people live a microwave lifestyle, they avoid preparation for a task or job. Lazy people have food all around them, but they are too lazy to see or use their resources. Our relationship with God requires motivation and conviction.

Reader's Thoughts:

- August 5 -

If you stop listening to instructions, my child,
you will turn your back on knowledge.
Proverbs 19:27

Author's Thoughts:

Knowledge flows and is always available. It is foolish to think that you are so wise that you stop listening to wisdom. Put a pause on your mindset about wisdom so that you can see wisdom in others. Is it not more important that your actions speak wisdom and others see you as wise rather than you thinking you are wise?

Reader's Thoughts:

- August 6 -

Those too lazy to plow in the right season will have no food at the harvest.

Proverbs 20:4

Author's Thoughts:

Your faith might be seasonal at times, but keep believing. You will find yourself in the right season just stay on track. Staying in the right season in your faith journey will require commitment and dedication to growing in your relationship with Jesus. Jesus will teach you that His faith is not seasonal, it is continual and consistent. The seasons come with doubt. Living a consistent faith journey with seasons is amazing.

Reader's Thoughts:

- August 7 -

Though good advice lies deep within the heart,
a person with understanding will draw it out.
Proverbs 20:5

Author's Thoughts:

An understanding of scripture and an intimate relationship with God makes for a really good view of spiritual direction. It is important that we elevate our knowledge and understanding so that we have good judgement and can acknowledge good advice, so not to ever get confused by poor advice. We must be equipped with solid judgment because the devil never stops trying to confuse us.

Reader's Thoughts:

- August 8 -

Many will say they are loyal friends,
but who can find one who is truly reliable?
Proverbs 20:6

Author's Thoughts:

A reliable and loyal friend has and expresses the spirit of truth and not the spirit of deception. Using discernment in selecting friends requires wisdom. We can trust in God's guidance and His gentle voice. It is better to have one Christ-like friend than to have a hundred friends who you can't trust their actions.

Reader's Thoughts:

- August 9 -

The Godly walk with integrity; blessed are their children who follow them.

Proverbs 20:7

Author's Thoughts:

When Elihu, our son, went off to college, I gave him one piece of advice and that was, "Son, guard your integrity." Our world is suffering from the lack of men and women with integrity. The kind of integrity that motivates love and respect for mankind. The kind of integrity that guides you to treating others "as Jesus so loves you." The kind of integrity that corrects wrongs and is patient enough to work with others who are struggling in their Christian journeys. I pray that we all live to guard our level of integrity, the kind of integrity that is acceptable in God's eyes.

Reader's Thoughts:

- August 10 -

Who can say, "I have cleansed my heart; I am pure and free from sin"?

Proverbs 20:9

Author's Thoughts:

God's discipline is righteous. If you have God's spirit in you, your sins will be forgiven. I know I am not living my life fully as Jesus expects, but I trust in His mercy and grace. I trust in His forgiving power. I trust in His hope for my life. I trust that He will remain in my heart and that because of that, I will not cause others to stumble. I trust in God's faith in me.

Reader's Thoughts:

- August 11 -

Even children are known by the way they act,
whether their conduct is pure, and whether it is right.
Proverbs 20:11

Author's Thoughts:

Our grandson, Isaiah, can be energetic at times, he is only seven years old. I am sure others have judged him when he seems out of control in public places. Since I get to experience the whole of Isaiah, my stance for him is different from those who might witness the worst in him. I am so thankful that the best in Isaiah outweighs his random energetic outbursts. I am so very thankful that God sees Isaiah's heart and will be patient with him in his life journey. I am so thankful that God's love for Isaiah is deeper than his Nana's love.

Reader's Thoughts:

- August 12 -

Ears to hear and eyes to see—both are gifts from the Lord.

Proverbs 20:12

Author's Thoughts:

It can be overwhelming, at times, to filter what your eyes see and your ears hear. God gives us so much to hear and see. Much of what we hear and see can be used to satisfy our own desires if we leave God out of these two gifts. God encourages us to listen to the downtrodden and witness His love for the oppressed. The weaknesses in what you hear or see can be turned into strengths. Jesus is available to help you recognize the good in all that you hear and see.

Reader's Thoughts:

- August 13 -

If you love sleep, you will end in poverty.
Keep your eyes open, and there will be plenty to eat!
Proverbs 20:13

Author's Thoughts:

Keep your eyes open for a love opportunity to speak to others through your faith. Sharing Jesus requires us to get up and open our eyes to see the needs of others. It requires us to serve and love the less fortunate. It requires us to love those who can be difficult to love. It requires us to forgive and love those who offend us. God's love allows us to move in a direction of love with our eyes open.

Reader's Thoughts:

- August 14 -

Wise words are more valuable than much gold and many rubies.

Proverbs 20:15

Author's Thoughts:

Surround yourself with people who have shown through their words and actions to be wise. If you can trace and evaluate their actions and that leads you to concluding that they sincerely seek God and they live in the spirit of truth, you can depend on their wisdom. Words and thoughts are powerful, always use good judgement in determining who you consider wise.

Reader's Thoughts:

- August 15 -

Stolen bread tastes sweet, but it turns to gravel in the mouth.

Proverbs 20:17

Author's Thoughts:

Sin can feel good, but it turns to evil quickly. Sin is short-lived, but God's grace and mercy lives forever. Sin leads you to dishonesty and can cause you to commit immoral and unlawful acts. God's love is eternal. The devil is weak; God is all powerful. The devil is unreliable; God can be trusted. There were times in my life that sin seemed so sweet to me, it was only enjoyable in the moment. The consequences of that short-lived enjoyment were measurable. Thanks be to God for His forgiving power.

Reader's Thoughts:

- August 16 -

Plans succeed through good counsel; don't go to war without wise advice.

Proverbs 20:18

Author's Thoughts:

When I look back over my life, I can clearly identify many times I went to war without sound wise advice and without praying for direction on how to battle. I can also clearly see the results of the times I battled with God's armor. I recognize God's love and forgiveness in the results of the wars without prayer. Life has taught me that God has the armor for all my battles even the ones that leave me weak.

Reader's Thoughts:

- August 17 -

A gossip goes around telling secrets, so don't hang around with chatterers.

Proverbs 20:19

Author's Thoughts:

Don't think that because you have a relationship with God that you won't find yourself in the middle of a conversation with hell raisers. When you do, just be that bright light that redirects the conversation or leaves the conversation. Correcting a hell raiser requires actions over time and sometimes from a distance. People who gossip tend to gossip until their own lives are impacted poorly by another hell raiser.

Reader's Thoughts:

- August 18 -

An inheritance obtained too early in life is not a blessing in the end.

Proverbs 20:21

Author's Thoughts:

I am reminded of an inheritance that is not monetary. It is important to have maturity and monetary instincts when you receive a monetary inheritance, if not, the blessing can easily turn into a curse. I am thankful for an inheritance of love from my parents. It was my parents who loved me well and taught me how to love others well. It is scripture that I embrace as an adult that motivates me to love others well. God is simply doing what God has commanded.

Reader's Thoughts:

- August 19 -

When the godly succeed, everyone is glad.
When the wicked take charge, people go into hiding.
Proverbs 28:12

Author's Thoughts:

My heart is overjoyed when I witness the godly achieve the mission of discipleship. Sharing the word and godly life with others is an act of service. The word is good and its application brings gladness to souls. When the godly take charge, souls are saved, and Jesus comes alive.

Reader's Thoughts:

- August 20 -

Don't say, "I will get even for this wrong."

Wait for the Lord to handle the matter.

Proverbs 20:22

Author's Thoughts:

Prayer and commitment to love are two attributes that encourage our hearts to forgive and not be inclined to get even. God expects us Christians to do good as His children. He expects our faith to be expressed in our responses to wrong. Waiting on God to handle evil can be challenging at times, but waiting is a true test of the depth of our faithfulness.

Reader's Thoughts:

- August 21 -

The Lord detest double standards; he is not pleased by dishonest scales.

Proverbs 20:23

Author's Thoughts:

We must be careful not to judge the sins of our neighbor. We are all sinners in need of God's mercy, grace, love, and forgiveness. Apparently, we are okay judging our fellow mankind until mankind takes the place of Jesus and judges us. How can a sinner fairly judge another sinner? Let Jesus, who knew no sin, examine our sins and provide fair and just consequences free from double standards.

Reader's Thoughts:

- August 22 -

Don't' trap yourself by making a rash promise to God
and only later counting the cost.
Proverbs 20:25

Author's Thoughts:

If we are unable to take responsibility for our mistakes, the power of learning from our own mistakes can be overlooked and not considered in future decisions. Making promises to God that have no thought process and no prayer consideration will cause defeat. God is all knowing and all loving; He sees your weaknesses. Trust in Him and in His faithfulness. You will need Him to fulfill your promises to Him.

Reader's Thoughts:

- August 23 -

The Lord's light penetrates the human spirit, exposing every hidden motive.

Proverbs 20:27

Author's Thoughts:

Lord, please penetrate my heart with your light. Please expose my un-Christ-like motives for me to see and be with me while my heart is being changed so that I can love the way you love. Lord please forgive me for my wrongs and never leave my side. Lord thanks for knowing my heart. Amen!

Reader's Thoughts:

- August 24 -

The glory of the young is their strength;

the gray hair of experience is the splendor of the old.

Proverbs 20:29

Author's Thoughts:

Well, not only am I considered a senior citizen, my hair is graying fast. Aging in my faith journey has inspired me to trust my journey. God has me on my individual faith journey that is designed for me. I totally agree that experience and age can be magnificent. What an opportunity to apply your life lessons and scripture teachings to how you live in your faith journey.

Reader's Thoughts:

- August 25 -

People may be right in their own eyes, but the Lord examines their heart.

Proverbs 21:2

Author's Thoughts:

God's ways and thoughts are unlike ours. We can't count the times in our lives that we behaved in ways that were acceptable to our own eyes, but unacceptable to God. We must be careful not to praise our own actions, but instead let God determine the praise. God sees when our actions are not in line with a loving heart. He also sees when the best in us is played out in our heart.

Reader's Thoughts:

- August 26 -

The Lord is more pleased when we do what is right
and just than when we offer him sacrifices.
Proverbs 21:3

Author's Thoughts:

During Lenten time, I normally give up coffee. What a personal sacrifice? I would be fooling myself if I try to connect it to something regarded as more important. The sacrifice doesn't encourage prayer and it has no positive affect on my relationship with Jesus. To be honest, I can't remember offering a sacrifice to God; I think the sacrifices were all for me. What I know for sure is that I try to do what is right, and when I do wrong, I ask for forgiveness and repent. Come to think of it, when I sacrifice for others, I sacrifice for God.

Reader's Thoughts:

- August 27 -

Haughty eyes, a proud heart, and evil actions are all sin.

Proverbs 21:4

Author's Thoughts:

For those who are quick to judge obvious sin and look down on other sinners, this verse is for you. It reminds us that sin that is unhindered causes damage to others. A proud heart can lead you down a destructive path without any recognition of wrong. It is extremely difficult for a proud heart to admit hurt or harm to others. It is not possible to change a proud heart if pride gets in the way of self-evaluation.

Reader's Thoughts:

- August 28 -

Good planning and hard work lead to prosperity,
but hasty shortcuts lead to poverty.
Proverbs 21:5

Author's Thoughts:

Portions of my life were filled with hasty decisions. I made financial decisions without a thought process and without applying the wisdom supplied by God. I worked hard but failed to plan accordingly. I was quick to blame my husband for poor money management, but I used him as an excuse not to manage with wisdom the abundance God provided. Thanks be to God, He provided. Thanks be to God, I learned from many financial planning mistakes and those lessons gave me a better perspective on investing and saving. I pray that my openness will encourage you to plan with wisdom.

Reader's Thoughts:

- August 29 -

The guilty walk a crooked path; the innocent travel a straight road.

Proverbs 21:8

Author's Thoughts:

Our God is awesome. His word teaches our heart the difference between a straight Christ-like path and a path filled with sin and guilt. He opens our conscience to an immediate Christ-like response, but He also gives us the decision to make choices. We can disregard His gentle guidance or we can regard evil. A thankful heart appreciates God's awesomeness.

Reader's Thoughts:

- August 30 -

It's better to live alone in the corner of an attic
than with a quarrelsome wife in a lovely home.
Proverbs 21:9

Author's Thoughts:

I was raised in a home with a mother, a father, four brothers, and four sisters. Our home was filled with quarrelsome people, but my mom wasn't one of them. Most wouldn't have called our home lovely, but most would agree that my mom was close to a Saint. I was the child that avoided attention and was comfortable in the corner. God is great; there is nobody greater than God.

Reader's Thoughts:

- August 31 -

A secret gift calms anger; a bribe under the table pacifies fury.

Proverbs 21:14

Author's Thoughts:

The most appreciated gift, in my opinion, is the one that is given in secret. Given not as a bribe, but a gift from a precious heart motivated by the heart of Jesus. I respect the gift of wise words with a foundation of love. I am so thankful for a loving family and friends that check my ways.

Reader's Thoughts:

~ September ~

Giving from a humble heart is freeing.

- September 1 -

Justice is a joy to the godly, but it terrifies evildoers.

Proverbs 21:15

Author's Thoughts:

God is truly just and fair. For those who have no sense of shame and have closed minds, God is just. For those who have gentle spirits and strong faith, God is just. For those who have hardened their hearts against right, God is just. For those with humble hearts, God is just. For those who believe that Jesus knows our thoughts and intentions, God is just.

Reader's Thoughts:

- September 2 -

Watch your tongue and keep your mouth shut, and you will stay out of trouble.

Proverb 21:23

Author's Thoughts:

God favors the humble, those who take the humble position of servers. Sometimes a position of humbleness requires us to listen without responding. Knowing when to be silent requires patience, discernment, and the application of wisdom. My personal experiences have taught me that the best response to some acts or words is silence. Your opinion is not always wise, not always needed, and not always appreciated. A silent response decreases your chances of getting into verbal trouble.

Reader's Thoughts:

- September 3 -

Some people are always greedy for more, but the godly love to give!

Proverb 21:26

Author's Thoughts:

It makes my heart emotionally uncomfortable when I take advantage of God's gifts or see someone else take advantage of His gifts. Greed interferes with the journey of a giver. Our thoughts are confused when mixed with thoughts associated with greed. It is wonderful to acknowledge when God gives us abundance and it is wonderful to give. Giving from a humble heart is freeing.

Reader's Thoughts:

- September 4 -

A false witness will be cut off, but a credible witness will be allowed to speak.

Proverbs 21:28

Author's Thoughts:

Waiting on God requires patience, diligence, understanding, and faith. How often do we listen to information and details that are not true, but refuse to speak truth? Holding back without defending a personal verbal wrong is exercising control. Instead of using your position of correctness, pray that God will reveal the truth and that the truth will cover you.

Reader's Thoughts:

- September 5 -

No human wisdom or understanding or plan can stand against the Lord.

Proverbs 21:30

Author's Thoughts:

It is not possible to please God without faith. It takes faith to believe that you or any other human can't stand in opposition to God and win the battle. If you wander off in your faith journey, God will not leave you. He stands by waiting for you to stand tall in your faith journey, but never stand against God. If you are true to your faith, God will provide the wisdom of understanding.

Reader's Thoughts:

- September 6 -

The horse is prepared for the day of battle, but the victory belongs to the Lord.

Proverbs 21:31

Author's Thoughts:

Your faith is a victory for Jesus Christ. Your spirit of power and self-discipline is a victory for Jesus Christ. When you live holy that is a victory for Jesus Christ. When you teach the good news, it is a victory for Jesus Christ. When you love your neighbor and love Jesus that is a victory for Jesus Christ. Jesus loves to open the doors to eternity.

Reader's Thoughts:

- September 7 -

Choose a good reputation over great riches;
being held in high esteem is better than silver or gold.
Proverbs 22:1

Author's Thoughts:

Developing and maintaining a good reputation is a personal choice. If your reputation is worthy of one who is held in high esteem for living a good life, God is pleased. Mankind tends to hold people in high esteem for a high dollar bank account, for a huge expensive house, or for a fancy, high-priced vehicle. God examines our hearts and how well we love. I would prefer for my reputation to be based on what is important to God rather than mankind.

Reader's Thoughts:

- September 8 -

The rich and poor have this in common: The Lord made them both.

Proverbs 22:2

Author's Thoughts:

What a blessing that we all start out equal in God's eyes whether we are rich or poor. We can all make God smile by living holy lives. Living our lives honoring and taking care of the less fortunate, living our lives loving our neighbors, living our lives to satisfy God's desires, and living our lives with God's spirit in our hearts is pleasing to God. Our lives are blessed with God as our father.

Reader's Thoughts:

- September 9 -

A prudent person foresees danger and takes precautions.
The simpleton goes blindly on and suffers the consequences.
Proverbs 22:3

Author's Thoughts:

I have learned life lessons from being accountable for bad decisions and consequences from bad decisions. These lessons are somewhat responsible for precautionary actions and measured thoughts. I am less of a simpleton and more of a prudent person now. I am thankful for growth in my faith journey.

Reader's Thoughts:

- September 10 -

True humility and fear of the Lord lead to riches, honor, and long life.

Proverbs 22:4

Author's Thoughts:

I have a humble spirit because I love and fear the Lord. My heart is rich in love. I honor my faith in Jesus. I am thankful for my life as it is, and I look forward to many more opportunities to honor God through service. I am a sinner saved by the blood of Jesus Christ. I am thankful for salvation.

Reader's Thoughts:

- September 11 -

Direct your children onto the right path,
and when they are older, they will not leave it.
Proverbs 22:6

Author's Thoughts:

I know many parents that are counting on their children coming back to a life of a right and good path. The path that God laid out for them and the path that their parents encouraged them to follow. We all stray away from a holy path at times, but we wake up quickly and move on in forgiveness. We all want the same forgiveness for our children. God is in our children waiting for them to trust His word and power. Keep being a holy example for your children and never stop praying. God is faithful.

Reader's Thoughts:

- September 12 -

Just as the rich rule the poor, so the borrower is servant to the lender.

Proverbs 22:7

Author's Thoughts:

We are, in some ways, all ruled by people who are in power, people who are richer, people who abuse our love, people who lend money or goods to us, people who manage us on the job, and people who we depend on for goods and services. It is important to always carry the knowledge that God is the almighty and that no one is more powerful.

Reader's Thoughts:

- September 13 -

Blessed are those who are generous, because they feed the poor.

Proverbs 22:9

Author's Thoughts:

God provides abundance to some and less to others so that the power of generosity can be expressed through God's love. Feeding the poor or the less fortunate is a visible example of the spirit of giving. We Christians are commanded to love our neighbors. Love is a powerful action word.

Reader's Thoughts:

- September 14 -

Whoever loves a pure heart and gracious speech will have the king as a friend.

Proverbs 22:11

Author's Thoughts:

Babies are born with pure hearts. We pray for pure hearts. The devil is alive and he uses mankind to change the hearts of babies. God is all powerful and He uses mankind to reveal His power to the devil. The devil's power is in competition with mankind. The devil has the power of an ant compared to God's power of eternity.

Reader's Thoughts:

- September 15 -

A youngster's heart is filled with foolishness,
but physical discipline will drive it far away.
Proverbs 22:15

Author's Thoughts:

God's love and protection will teach you the endurance required to rid your thoughts of foolishness. Physical discipline starts with our thoughts. How we think and what we allow in our thoughts determines our mental and physical maturity. Some of us live our entire lives with hearts of youngsters. Applying scripture to our daily lives and decisions moves us into the maturity of salvation.

Reader's Thoughts:

- September 16 -

Don't rob the poor just because you can, or exploit the needy in court. For the Lord is their defender. He will ruin anyone who ruins them.

Proverbs 22:22-23

Author's Thoughts:

Scripture is clear, God defends and protects the poor and needy. Jesus can be found in the poor and needy. We miss out on a Jesus experience when we disregard and not offer love to the poor and needy. The poor are always in need of basic life "stuff." The needy can be in need of a hug, a smile, love, attention, forgiveness, or a kind word. The needy can be rich in money and the poor can be rich in love.

Reader's Thoughts:

- September 17 -

Don't befriend angry people or associate with hot-tempered people,
or you will learn to be like them and endanger your soul.
Proverbs 22:24-25

Author's Thoughts:

Before I gained knowledge of what God expects from me as a follower of Jesus, I was hot-tempered and my responses at times were hurtful. I pray that my actions never endangered the soul of any human being. When I offend God in my actions, words, or thoughts, I go to Him with an open heart prepared to accept His forgiveness. I no longer behave with a hot-temper, but at times, I catch myself using scripture to defend the indefensible. God please forgive me. Amen!

Reader's Thoughts:

- September 18 -

Don't wear yourself out trying to get rich. Be wise enough to know when to quit.
In the blink of an eye wealth disappears,
for it will sprout wings and fly away like an eagle.
Proverbs 23:4-5

Author's Thoughts:

What a valuable lesson. So many of us live our lives trying to get rich instead of trying to treat others with respect and dignity. God's love is dependable, and it will never fly away. God has the power to supply all our needs and His love brings joy and happiness. Your faith saves, your faith brings riches, and your faith supports a life of abundance. We are all rich in God's love and are given an opportunity to have an abundant life in Jesus.

Reader's Thoughts:

- September 19 -

Don't waste your breath on fools, for they will despise the wisest advice.

Proverbs 23:9

Author's Thoughts:

If God blessed you with wisdom and you are not afraid to be wise, please use good judgment when you speak wisdom and who you speak wisdom to. Fools will dislike you for your wisdom because they decided to disregard God's teachings in their lives. Wisdom is better expressed, at times, through your actions. It is more challenging for fools to despise you for your actions than for your advice.

Reader's Thoughts:

- September 20 -

Commit yourself to instruction; listen carefully to words of knowledge.

Proverbs 23:12

Author's Thoughts:

For the young and the old, please listen to God's wisdom. He will speak to you in a gentle voice. Please don't give up when God corrects you, His discipline is divine. Please trust in God's love. I am not sure when it happened, but a few years ago God spoke to me about valuing my own thoughts. Now I know that my thoughts can be inspiring and that my thoughts are valuable to others. Your thoughts are words of Knowledge, make your thoughts stimulating.

Reader's Thoughts:

- September 21 -

Don't fail to discipline your children. They won't die if you spank them. Physical discipline may well save them from death.

Proverbs 23:13-14

Author's Thoughts:

I have three children who are all adults. My husband and I didn't practice physical discipline as a means for disciplining our children, but there were times when physical discipline was warranted. I think that physical discipline should be a last resort and that the physical discipline shouldn't be corporal punishment. Discipline is designed to reinforce good behavior, not to demean others. I believe in taking away things that children enjoy, or not giving them things that they enjoy, when they exhibit poor behavioral traits. I also believe in a gentle discussion about consequences for actions.

Reader's Thoughts:

- September 22 -

My child, if your heart is wise, my own heart will rejoice.

Proverbs 23:15

Author's Thoughts:

God's gentle voice always lets me know when my actions and words are not of a wise heart. It makes my heart rejoice when I know God is pleased with my heart. I am forever thankful for the opportunity to be wise and to encourage wisdom in others.

Reader's Thoughts:

- September 23 -

Everything in me will celebrate when you speak what is right.

Proverbs 23:16

Author's Thoughts:

Imagine Jesus celebrating when His people speak and do what is right. What we say and how we speak it matters to our neighbors. God sometimes uses us to save a fellow soul by the words we express. We must exercise self-control and consider our thoughts before speaking. Wisdom requires self-control. Let's all pray to speak words that encourage others to want to know Jesus.

Reader's Thoughts:

- September 24 -

Don't envy sinners, but always continue to fear the Lord.
You will be rewarded for this; your hope will not be disappointed.
Proverbs 23:17-18

Author's Thoughts:

If we are not careful, we can envy others because they have materialistic things that we do not have, but want. If we are not careful, the people we envy will convince us to step outside of Jesus' teachings to acquire that which we envy. Keep hope alive, God will supply all your needs. Don't make the mistake of sinning for a want or desire.

Reader's Thoughts:

- September 25 -

My child, listen and be wise: Keep your heart on the right course.

Proverbs 28:19

Author's Thoughts:

God clearly teaches us to be wise. Our hearts must be wrapped in faith to be protected from evil. God wants us to do what we teach children to do and that is love others and be wise in our decisions. In order to stay on a faith track, our hearts must be considerate and loving.

Reader's Thoughts:

- September 26 -

Get the truth and never sell it; also get wisdom, discipline, and good judgment.

Proverbs 23:23

Author's Thoughts:

Now, my life is a product of when and how I allowed my heart to grow in wisdom. When I recognized the importance and benefits of discipline and discernment, my actions and thought patterns took on a different intensity of love. Blessings flow when you slow down and appreciate truth.

Reader's Thoughts:

- September 27 -

The father of godly children has cause for joy.
What a pleasure to have children who are wise.
Proverbs 23:24

Author's Thoughts:

I must show appreciation to God by how I apply scripture to my life journey. I am thankful for godly children. My three children are all loving and considerate. They were all introduced to God at very young ages and they all believe that Christ died on the cross for our sins. They all know that salvation is available to them. I witness my children grow in wisdom and that makes me a proud mom.

Reader's Thoughts:

- September 28 -

So give your father and mother joy. May she who give you birth be happy.

Proverbs 23:25

Author's Thoughts:

I am happy when my mother is pleased with me. My mother is happy when I please God. I am happy when my children love others. My children are happy when I don't allow anything or anyone to steal my joy. My father passed away in 1983, the same year Phillip and I married. I am thankful that I know that I pleased my father.

Reader's Thoughts:

- September 29 -

The godly care about the rights of the poor; the wicked don't care at all.

Proverbs 29:7

Author's Thoughts:

The rights and needs of the poor are important to Jesus and it must be important to His followers. We who follow Jesus are expected to love our neighbors including the poor and needy. Love comes with care, support, and understanding for our fellow mankind. It is wise to acknowledge and act on the needs of the poor and to protect the rights of the poor.

Reader's Thoughts:

- September 30 -

O my son, give me your heart. May your eyes take delight in following my ways.

Proverbs 23:26

Author's Thoughts:

Give God your heart, mind, and soul. He can be trusted with all of you. God is so pleased when we delight in His ways. When your faith is shaken, go out and help someone less fortunate than you. God will show up in your helping hands and comfort you in your faith. When your faith is shaken, love deeper and stay hopeful. God will reveal his love and commitment through your weakest moments. God is faithful even when our faith is tested.

Reader's Thoughts:

Reader's Thoughts:

October

Knowledge is the key to understanding
why you believe in Jesus Christ.

- October 1 -

Don't envy evil people or desire their company.

For their hearts plot violence, and their words always stir up trouble.

Proverbs 24:1-2

Author's Thoughts:

We are required to use good judgement so that God can reveal the ways of evil people. Knowledge of God's truth and the application of His truth can ward off people who live their lives to create trouble for themselves and others. God's truth is your armor of protection against evil people.

Reader's Thoughts:

- October 2 -

A house is built by wisdom and becomes strong through good sense.
Through knowledge its rooms are filled with all sorts
of precious riches and valuables.
Proverbs 24:3-4

Author's Thoughts:

Phillip and I were married for 26 years; we loved for 38 years. He passed away on November 22, 2017 at 12:30 PM EST. His children and I were with him as he took his last breath and opened his eyes to Jesus. Most of our 26 years of marriage were in a home not built on wisdom nor did we rely on God's strength. Yes, we both believed that Jesus died on the cross for our sins. We struggled with the application of the word. I am thankful that even with our struggles, we always believed in the unseen, and we acknowledged that we were both sinners saved by God. If you struggle with applying the word, keep trying. Keep believing.

Reader's Thoughts:

- October 3 -

The wise are mightier than the strong,
and those with knowledge grow stronger and stronger.
Proverbs 24:5

Author's Thoughts:

Knowledge is the key to understanding why you believe in Jesus Christ. The more you grow in knowledge, the stronger your faith will become. Knowledge of the word and strong faith enhances joy through hope. Wisdom is divine, it can move mountains to allow you to see Jesus clearer.

Reader's Thoughts:

- October 4 -

If you fail under pressure, your strength is too small.

Proverbs 24:10

Author's Thoughts:

At times, it seems that people who love Jesus are under more pressure than those who don't know Jesus. In those moments, we should remind ourselves of God's sacrifice of giving up His son, Jesus Christ, for our sins. Remind ourselves that we can be made righteous because God released the pressure of sin through His only son. If you find that your strength is not sufficient, that probably means that you left the strength and power of Jesus out of your decision making and action power. God's strength will always be sufficient.

Reader's Thoughts:

- October 5 -

The godly may trip seven times, but they will get up again.
But one disaster is enough to overthrow the wicked.
Proverbs 24:16

Author's Thoughts:

You are a living witness that the godly just keep standing trial after trial. The godly will never be overthrown in Jesus. We witness trials turn into joy every day of our lives. We witness people getting up and dusting themselves off from the death of loved ones, loss of a home, job loss, sickness, addiction, lost love, etc. God is our most powerful counselor. Let Jesus Christ hold your hand and carry you when you feel you can't take another step.

Reader's Thoughts:

- October 6 -

Don't rejoice when your enemies fall; don't be happy when they stumble.
For the Lord will be displeased with you and will turn his anger away from them.
Proverbs 24:17-18

Author's Thoughts:

Pray for our enemies and wish them well. God is pleased when we love those who are difficult to love. God is pleased when we pray for those who wish evil for us. God's light shines through His people when they love their enemies. You can save a soul by how you love. Your love can motivate a soul to get to know Jesus Christ.

Reader's Thoughts:

- October 7 -

An honest answer is like a kiss of friendship.

Proverbs 24:26

Author's Thoughts:

We must use diplomacy even in honest answers. An honest response can sometimes cause harm if it is not delivered with love, consideration, and in most cases, compassion. Not all of your friends or family can deal with straight forward, honest responses. Some of our friends require diplomacy even in our actions. As long as your responses are delivered with love, please make them honest and straight forward. Remember the honest truth is painful to some, so be prepared for your responses to sometimes be rejected.

Reader's Thoughts:

- October 8 -

Do your planning and prepare your fields before building your house.

Proverbs 24:27

Author's Thoughts:

So many of us build our surroundings without any planning or preparation. We are quick to be disappointed and may even blame God for our lack of planning. How can you build a journey of faith without scripture knowledge? How can you build a solid home without a foundation? Be patient in your planning and talk with God along the way. Learn to listen to God's gentle voice and be guided by His voice.

Reader's Thoughts:

- October 9 -

Remove the wicked from the King's court,
and his reign will be made secure by justice.
Proverbs 25:5

Author's Thoughts:

If your heart is wicked, you must allow Jesus to take the place of the wickedness in your heart. Your heart drives your thoughts and your thoughts drive your actions. The devil has power and we must consider the devil's power so that we are clearly motivated to rely on the most powerful, Jesus Christ. The devil has a way of entering our thoughts during our weakest moments. We can teach the devil to stay out of our thoughts by consistently introducing him to Jesus Christ. When you consistently rely on Jesus' power and strength, the devil will stay away from you.

Reader's Thoughts:

- October 10 -

It's better to wait for an invitation to the head table
than to be sent away in public disgrace.
Proverbs 25:7

Author's Thoughts:

I often find myself at the head of a table even when it makes me uncomfortable. Sometimes I am sent away, but not in disgrace because I don't sit at the head of any table without being invited. I am most comfortable being at the back of the room listening to those with knowledge. It may be that individuals at the head of the table should be equipped with profound knowledge and wisdom. It is important to know your place before you walk into a room.

Reader's Thoughts:

- October 11 -

Just because you've seen something, don't be in a hurry to go to court.
For what will you do in the end if your neighbor deals you a shameful defeat?
Proverbs 25:8

Author's Thoughts:

It is important that we teach our minds not to respect all that we see or hear. In most circumstances, the information is received for our own personal growth and it is not meant to be shared with anyone other than God. Repeating information in a hurry doesn't give us time for discernment. Repeating details with poor judgement will surely hurt someone else.

Reader's Thoughts:

- October 12 -

When arguing with your neighbor, don't betray another person's secret.

Proverbs 25:9

Author's Thoughts:

Secrets are told in confidence. Most secrets are communicated in personal confidence. If you must tell secrets let them be your own. When someone trusts you enough to share intimate secrets, be loyal to secrecy, don't betray a relationship because you violated your neighbor's trust.

Reader's Thoughts:

- October 13 -

Timely advice is lovely, like golden apples in a silver basket.

Proverbs 25:11

Author's Thoughts:

I love constructive advice that's timely. I respect the advice of wise people and I can handle brutal wisdom. I don't have the patience for people who give advice on topics or issues that are clearly not their forte. Seek advice from people who have a proven record in your area of concern or need.

Reader's Thoughts:

- October 14 -

Trustworthy messengers refresh like snow in summer.
They revive the spirit of their employer.
Proverbs 25:13

Author's Thoughts:

Loyal and trustworthy people refresh and enhance the lives of all who share their space. We all need loyal and trustworthy individuals in our life circles. These individuals normally have clear characteristics of wisdom and godly knowledge. People who are loyal and faithful to the Holy Spirit can be trusted with your most prized possessions and with your love. They can be trusted to apply the word to their messages and actions.

Reader's Thoughts:

- October 15 -

A person who promises a gift but doesn't give it
is like clouds and wind that bring no rain.
Proverbs 25:14

Author's Thoughts:

Be a person of integrity. Be a person that can be trusted. Be an upstanding honest soul. Be dedicated to the word and its application. Be a person of God. Be committed to knowledge. Be diligent in your walk with Jesus. Be loyal to love. Be hopeful. Be that person who loves without conditions. Give the gift of wisdom to those who you share earthly space with.

Reader's Thoughts:

- October 16 -

Patience can persuade a prince, and soft speech can break bones.

Proverbs 25:15

Author's Thoughts:

Patience requires prayer talks with Jesus. Patience requires you to exercise self-control. Patience requires you to have a thought process before speaking or acting. Patience requires us to acknowledge God's grace. Patience makes soft speech possible. Soft speech can change a hardened heart.

Reader's Thoughts:

- October 17 -

Putting confidence in an unreliable person in times of trouble is like chewing with a broken tooth or walking on a lame foot.

Proverbs 25:19

Author's Thoughts:

How many times have we done something for someone we knew weren't reliable, but turned around and blamed them for not living up to their promises? How many times have we discussed intimate details of our lives with people who we knew couldn't be trusted and turned our backs on them when they repeated the intimate details? You should expect pain, not disappointment, when you deal with someone who already proved through their action that they can't be trusted.

Reader's Thoughts:

- October 18 -

Singing cheerful songs to a person with a heavy heart is like taking someone's coat in cold weather or pouring vinegar in a wound.

Proverbs 25:20

Author's Thoughts:

When my heart is heavy, I need a trusted friend to listen and comfort me with stories of people who are overcomers. I love hearing about and witnessing hope come alive in our daily walks with Jesus. I love having friends call me with scripture references when my heart is heavy or my faith is fading. Your friends with heavy hearts need to be reminded of God's grace and mercy displayed in their lives.

Reader's Thoughts:

It's not good to eat too much honey,
and it's not good to seek honors for yourself.
Proverbs 25:27

Author's Thoughts:

It is an indescribable feeling when you are recognized for things you do that are simply part of who God made you. Being honored for being you is a demonstration of God's grace. There is no need to honor yourself if you have faith in Jesus Christ. Jesus can be trusted to touch the hearts of others when honor is deserved and important enough to be visualized. It is important that others are allowed to honor you and it is important to accept the honor with grace and a thankful heart.

Reader's Thoughts:

- October 20 -

If your enemies are hungry, give them food to eat.
If they are thirsty, give them water to drink.
Proverbs 25:21

Author's Thoughts:

Feed your enemies with kindness. Let your enemies experience God through your words and actions. Show a heart of forgiveness and the strength to love those whom you have forgiven. Some individuals are your enemies because they were never taught the value of friendship and love. Forgive your enemies and God will forgive you.

Reader's Thoughts:

- October 21 -

As surely as a north wind brings rain, so a gossiping tongue causes anger!

Proverbs 25:23

Author's Thoughts:

I never want to use my tongue as a gossiping weapon. No matter how much I try, I still find myself gossiping at times. In most cases, it is after the damage was done that I realized I allowed myself to be a part of gossip. I continue to pray for deliverance in this area. I am thankful that God sees my heart and judges me accordingly. Lord, I pray for those who are affected by gossip. I pray that they forgive their perpetrators and move on in God.

Reader's Thoughts:

- October 22 -

It's better to live alone in the corner of an attic
than with a quarrelsome wife in a lovely home.
Proverbs 25:24

Author's Thoughts:

Women, please do not be argumentative or confrontational with your husbands. Gentle and kind words will motivate change in both you and your spouse. Love him in a godly way without conditions. Forgive him for his shortcomings and move into the future. If you are feeling unloved, talk with your husband about your needs. Let your husband know your likes and dislikes. By all means, bring happiness to the marriage, do not burden your husband with the responsibility of making you happy. Love Well!

Reader's Thoughts:

- October 23 -

A person without self-control is like a city with broken-down walls.

Proverbs 25:28

Author's Thoughts:

We all have had moments without self-control. In those moments, it does feel like all the barriers around you have fallen down and you are left without emotional or physical protection. It is in those moments that Jesus is carrying you until you can carry yourself. God doesn't leave you unprotected; He is always available with strength, hope, protection, mercy, and love. Your brokenness is a meantime experience.

Reader's Thoughts:

- October 24 -

Honor is no more associated with fools than
snow with summer or rain with harvest.
Proverbs 26:1

Author's Thoughts:

Honor is special and honor comes with the responsibility of trust. Honor doesn't mean perfection, but it does require a person of distinction and one who is highly respected. It is my honor to be a child born to Mildred and Mack Crook. This honor comes with pride and respect and it gives me joy to know that God honored me with such wonderful and loving parents. Remember to honor those who honor you.

Reader's Thoughts:

- October 25 -

Don't answer the foolish arguments of fools,

or you will become as foolish as they are.

Proverbs 26:4

Author's Thoughts:

Being a fool will surprise you. I can't count the number of times I found myself in an argument with a foolish person doing foolish things. When I recognize that I am in foolish sin, I immediately calm my mind and thoughts and back out of the conversation. In some cases, I stayed in a foolish conversation too long which resulted in pain to others. My actions required an apology, repentance, and turning back to God for forgiveness. Foolish is as foolish does.

Reader's Thoughts:

- October 26 -

Honoring a fool is as foolish as tying a stone to a slingshot.

Proverbs 26:8

Author's Thoughts:

I respect the position of the President of the United States and I pray for the President's leadership and for his family. I think we all should be held accountable for our actions whether good or bad. It is the responsibility of the people to hold all Presidents accountable for their actions. I pray that we do not close our eyes to wrong, even when the wrong comes from our leaders.

Reader's Thoughts:

~ October 27 ~

There is more hope for fools than for people who think they are wise.

Proverbs 26:12

Author's Thoughts:

My heart is moved when other people see me as wise. I don't take their thoughts lightly. I am honored to be seen as wise and I understand that it places a special responsibility on me to act accordingly. I am hopeful because I don't see myself as wise, but I respect those who do. I am humbled to be called a woman of wisdom.

Reader's Thoughts:

- October 28 -

Interfering in someone else's argument is as foolish as yanking a dog's ears.

Proverbs 26:17

Author's Thoughts:

If you are not invited into an argument to help slow down the pace of offensive language, don't interfere. It is important to stay in your lane when you witness arguments and conflict. In most cases being a silent observer is appropriate. It is difficult to diffuse or offer advice to people who are in heated arguments. Foolish people invite themselves into an argument. Wise people offer help when needed.

Reader's Thoughts:

- October 29 -

Rumors are dainty morsels that sink deep into one's heart.

Proverbs 26:22

Author's Thoughts:

We are expected to be offended by rumors. We are expected to walk away from a rumored conversation. We are expected to defend, when appropriate, the people who are the source of rumors. We are expected to understand that rumors are destructive lies. We are expected to avoid those who have an established reputation to create rumors without any consideration for the impact rumors have on the hearts of others.

Reader's Thoughts:

- October 30 -

Smooth words may hide a wicked heart, just as a pretty glaze covers a clay pot.

Proverbs 26:23

Author's Thoughts:

Our world has no shortage of mankind with wicked hearts. Our world has no shortage of mankind with kind and considerate hearts. The good will always prevail over the wicked. God is good and He is in the hearts of mankind who are good. God can turn a wicked heart into good. It is our responsibility to exercise good judgement in examining the hearts of others.

Reader's Thoughts:

- October 31 -

People may cover their hatred with pleasant words, but they're deceiving you.

Proverbs 26:24

Author's Thoughts:

I am of the opinion that hatred is obvious, but sometimes it takes a minute for us to see through deceptive words or actions. Hatred will rear its ugly head no matter how hard the hater tries to conceal it. Being deceived by hate is short lived. If you trust in God, He will put a spotlight on deception. Love and hate are unlike in nature. The characteristics of hate are contrary to the characteristics of love. We shouldn't be easily fooled.

Reader's Thoughts:

November

The best reward for your faith journey
is to know that God is pleased with you.

- November 1 -

If you set a trap for others, you will get caught in it yourself.
If you roll a boulder down on others, it will crush you instead.
Proverbs 26:27

Author's Thoughts:

Loving, respectful, faithful, hopeful, forgiving, understanding, patient and thoughtful are God-like qualities that we should all treasure and pray that our neighbor values as well. If you wish evil on others, evil is sure to land at your feet. If you love your neighbor and you are quick to forgive, you will be loved, and others will be quick to forgive you.

Reader's Thoughts:

- November 2 -

A lying tongue hates its victims, and flattering words cause ruin.

Proverbs 26:28

Author's Thoughts:

Speaking with honesty is powerful and sometimes freeing. There shouldn't be any dishonesty even in flattering words. There are no positive benefits for one to embrace dishonesty. Why flatter people who are sinning? When you flatter them, you give credit to their wrongdoings. It should be easy to flatter people who are godly, but I find that godly people are not standing in line to be flattered. On the other hand, those who do evil love flattering remarks and flattering things.

Reader's Thoughts:

- November 3 -

Don't brag about tomorrow, since you don't know what the day will bring.

Proverbs 27:1

Author's Thoughts:

Now that I have an appreciation and an acknowledgement for every moment that I breathe, I have more of an understanding of the benefits of not bragging about tomorrow or worrying about tomorrow. My life journey has been full of wonderful times and sad times. In both good and not so good times, I learned to be patient in my faith journey. All things, yes, all things, have turned out for the good. I learned a great deal from making the mistake of worrying about things that I couldn't change or about things that never happened. Keep the faith.

Reader's Thoughts:

- November 4 -

A prudent person foresees danger and takes precautions.
The simpleton goes blindly on and suffers the consequences.
Proverbs 27:12

Author's Thoughts:

Some consequences are irreversible and part of God's plan for your life. We must learn to embrace the consequences of our ways and actions. If we appreciate good and positive consequences, we must live our lives in good and positive ways. Live a sensible life with wisdom as your foundation and be well advised in your decision making.

Reader's Thoughts:

- November 5 -

Let someone else praise you, not your own mouth– a stranger, not your own lips.

Proverbs 27:2

Author's Thoughts:

I have always been uncomfortable praising myself and most of the time I am uncomfortable when others praise me. I am thankful that God has me in a position to be praised. I am thankful that God is a forgiving God and He knows when I am not worthy of praise and that He forgives me of my shortcomings. I am thankful that others find me worthy of praise; I don't take their respect for granted. God is good.

Reader's Thoughts:

- November 6 -

A stone is heavy and sand is weighty,
but the resentment caused by a fool is even heavier.
Proverbs 27:3

Author's Thoughts:

We are all affected by foolish resentment. Sometimes, in order for God to teach a fool a lesson about resentment, He allows the wise to suffer the consequences of a fool's resentment. All of our hearts were designed to know wrong and to know when we wrong someone else. Jesus is in our hearts, we must learn to listen to His gentle voice. It is wrong to store up resentment because you will release that resentment in ways that cause pain to another person.

Reader's Thoughts:

- November 7 -

Anger is cruel, and wrath, is like a flood, but jealousy is even more dangerous.

Proverbs 27:4

Author's Thoughts:

Can you remember moments in your life where jealousy controlled your thoughts? Those were intolerable moments. We are not designed to bear the burden of jealousy. The weight of jealousy is demeaning for the person who is jealous and for the person who is affected by jealousy. Anger is a quick meantime experience, but jealousy stays in your heart for some time. God please allow anger and jealousy to escape from our hearts before the results impact others. Amen!

Reader's Thoughts:

- November 8 -

An open rebuke is better than hidden love!

Proverbs 27:5

Author's Thoughts:

Expressing disapproval of our wrong actions and the wrong actions of others is a form of expressing love and concern. There are some acts that must be immediately responded to with disapproval and sometimes criticism. Love can be found in fair and just criticism and consequences.

Reader's Thoughts:

- November 9 -

A person who strays from home is like a bird that strays from its nest.

Proverbs 27:8

Author's Thoughts:

Consider your marriage a home and never stray away. Treat your marriage as God intended, like a covenant with God, not a contract as defined by the world.

Reader's Thoughts:

- November 10 -

The heartfelt counsel of a friend is as sweet as perfume and incense.

Proverbs 27:9

Author's Thoughts:

Faithful and loyal friends are rare. If you have a couple of loyal friends, consider yourself blessed. You can count on trusted friends to be honest and to offer words of encouragements that are heartfelt. Give your friends the gift of trusted and wise counsel.

Reader's Thoughts:

- November 11 -

Never abandon a friend– either yours or your father's.

Proverbs 27:10a

Author's Thoughts:

Early in life, I developed a reputation of being a dependable and loving friend. I later developed a reputation of being a friend with wise advice, advice that is well thought out and measured. I treasure dependable and god-like friends. I treasure friends who are honest and who love me without conditions. I treasure friends who would never consider abandoning me in times of need. Good friends are immeasurable.

Reader's Thoughts:

- November 12 -

Be wise, my child, and make my heart glad.
Then I will be able to answer my critics.
Proverbs 27:11

Author's Thoughts:

Let's pray that our words and actions make God's heart glad. God is our healer. He is our rescuer. He is our counselor. He is our heavenly father. He is our friend. He is worthy of praise. The best reward for your faith journey is to know that God is pleased with you. God will answer your critics when you are godly.

Reader's Thoughts:

- November 13 -

As a face is reflected in water, so the heart reflects the real person.

Proverbs 27:19

Author's Thoughts:

Do you see yourself when you look into the mirror? Are you pleased with what you see? Do you examine your heart? Are you pleased with the truth of your heart? Are you prepared to change what you see in the mirror? Is your faith strong enough to let Jesus change your heart? Are you prepared to live a life that is dedicated to godly living? Answer these questions with truth.

Reader's Thoughts:

- November 14 -

Just as death and destruction are never satisfied,

so human desire is never satisfied.

Proverbs 27:20

Author's Thoughts:

The devil doesn't have a shortage of destruction or death. The devil understands that human desires are always open for abuse. The devil stands by waiting for an opportunity to take advantage of our weak desires. Jesus is the only answer to the ways of the devil. Jesus is all powerful and the devil is aware of His power. The problem with humans is that we sometimes have less confidence in Jesus' power than in the devil.

Reader's Thoughts:

- November 15 -

The wicked run away when no one is chasing them,
but the godly are as bold as lions.
Proverbs 28:1

Author's Thoughts:

Be bold and courageous in your faith. Share your faith with others with a fearless spirit. Don't let the wicked encourage you to turn your attention away from your faith. Let the wicked see Jesus through your faith journey. It is important to disciple in word, but it is more important to disciple through actions.

Reader's Thoughts:

- November 16 -

When there is moral rot within a nation, its government topples easily.
But wise and knowledgeable leaders bring stability.
Proverbs 28:2

Author's Thoughts:

One can argue that America's morality is under attack and if our people are not careful, morality will rot. Our values and principals are being tested by words and actions that contradict good. We are actually turning our backs on what is right because we dislike truth. We prepare our minds to believe in powerful and influential humans with a disregard to godly ways. Wrong can never be right no matter who is doing the wrong.

Reader's Thoughts:

- November 17 -

A poor person who oppresses the poor is like
a pounding rain that destroys the crops.
Proverbs 28:3

Author's Thoughts:

How can a poor person oppress another poor person? Why would a rich person treat another rich person unjustly? I think both answers are related to power and the fear of losing power or influence over people or circumstances. Oppression comes from fear of the abilities of the people you are oppressing. Oppression should be undesirable amongst the godly.

Reader's Thoughts:

- November 18 -

To reject the law is to praise the wicked; to obey the law is to fight them.

Proverbs 28:4

Author's Thoughts:

In order for us to fight the wicked, we must first acknowledge the wicked. In order for us to obey the law, we must first understand the law. When we understand the law, we can apply the law.

Reader's Thoughts:

- November 19 -

Evil people don't understand justice, but those
who follow the Lord understand completely.
Proverbs 28:5

Author's Thoughts:

Being just requires fairness of applied rules and laws. An understanding of rules and laws places a responsibility of conformity. Some of us spend our lives with full knowledge of rules and laws, but spend our brain space disregarding them. Those who are evil with a lack of understanding are judged according. Those who are evil with understanding knowledge are also judged accordingly.

Reader's Thoughts:

- November 20 -

Young people who obey the law are wise;
those with wild friends bring shame to their parents.
Proverbs 28:7

Author's Thoughts:

This is such a personal verse for me. One of my beautiful children doesn't have the discernment when it comes to friends. She is easily influenced and quick to say yes to things that are harmful to her body and soul. Obeying the law and applying wisdom to her decisions is secondary to her immediate needs. Prayer has sustained her and prayer will continue to sustain her until she believes in the power of godly ways.

Reader's Thoughts:

- November 21 -

God detests the prayers of a person who ignores the law.

Proverbs 28:9

Author's Thoughts:

It is important that godly people pray for sinners, including themselves. There shouldn't be anyone who is not covered in prayer. Jesus hears all of our prayers and He responds in due time. Please do not underestimate the power of prayer.

Reader's Thoughts:

- November 22 -

A hard worker has plenty of food, but a person
who chases fantasies ends up in poverty.
Proverbs 28:19

Author's Thoughts:

Chasing fantasies can be an addiction. Most, if not all, addictions are destructive and demeaning. Hard work is honorable and worthy of pride. Hard work brings a sense of achievement and gratification. Fantasies are improbable and warm the hearts of people who like to make believe.

Reader's Thoughts:

- November 23 -

Rich people may think they are wise, but a poor person with discernment can see right through them.

Proverbs 28:11

Author's Thoughts:

People tend to think that rich people are wise simply because they are rich. Wisdom is not always associated with wealth. Wisdom doesn't have a price tag on it. The value of wisdom far exceeds wealth. An abundance of wisdom can lead to an abundance of wealth, but not always. My preference is discernment over wealth because the gift of discernment can lead to godly wealth.

Reader's Thoughts:

- November 24 -

People who conceal their sins will not prosper,
but if they confess and turn from them, they will receive mercy.
Proverbs 28:13

Author's Thoughts:

Acknowledging sin is a form of freedom. Facing sin head on motivates prayer. Prayer is a stepstool to forgiveness. Prayer allows us to confess to the almighty Jesus Christ and to be considered for forgiveness. Forgiveness is a clear reflection of God's mercy.

Reader's Thoughts:

- November 25 -

Blessed are those who fear to do wrong,

but the stubborn are headed for serious trouble.

Proverbs 28:14

Author's Thoughts:

I am of the opinion that we must fear wrong for us to do right. Stubborn people who have no fear of God are not protected by His armor. God's armor of protection saves us from unwise actions and decisions. God's protection is promised and can be trusted.

Reader's Thoughts:

- November 26 -

A ruler with no understanding will oppress his people,
but one who hates corruption will have a long life.
Proverbs 28:16

Author's Thoughts:

A self-absorbed leader considers his/her own interests over the needs of his subordinates. This type of leader has no understanding of the needs and desires of the oppressed. Unethical conduct is a friend to a self-absorbed leader. A leader who rules with integrity has an understanding heart.

Reader's Thoughts:

The blameless will be rescued from harm,
but the crooked will be suddenly destroyed.
Proverbs 28:18

Author's Thoughts:

To be convinced that you will be saved from hurt and pain requires faith. It requires patience and diligence. When we see the crooked prosper, our faith should increase. God's consequences are just and timely. Believe that the faithful will be saved and protected.

Reader's Thoughts:

- November 28 -

The trustworthy person will get a rich reward,
but a person who wants quick riches will get into trouble.
Proverbs 28:20

Author's Thoughts:

If you have to violate a trusted relationship or cause pain to another human being to get rich, you are probably practicing greed. Disregarding God's plans for your life for monetary richness is like a slow death. You spend years in a position of stress and discomfort because God doesn't provide peace or joy when we are disregarding His purpose for our lives. There is a godly reward for trustworthiness and a commitment to doing what is right.

Reader's Thoughts:

- November 29 -

A proverb in the mouth of a fool is as useless as a paralyzed leg.

Proverbs 26:7

Author's Thoughts:

The Book of Proverbs is a source of wisdom and insight. The Book of Proverbs was written by a wise man. The wisdom revealed in the Book of Proverbs can be applied to our lives and is an excellent decision-making guide. This book of wisdom is not designed for fools.

Reader's Thoughts:

- November 30 -

Showing partiality is never good,
yet some will do wrong for a mere piece of bread.
Proverbs 28:21

Author's Thoughts:

The moment you take your eyes and mind off your faith journey, the devil is there to fill your mind with thoughts of regrets and unholy desires. The devil moves you away from being content to being confused. The devil causes you to be jealous of your friends and family. The devil causes you to be unfaithful in relationships. The devil will encourage your mind to think wrongly in spite of your faith in Jesus. In your weakest moments, always turn towards Jesus and away from worldly thoughts and things.

Reader's Thoughts:

- November 31 -

Greedy people try to get rich quick but don't realize they're headed for poverty.

Proverbs 28:22

Author's Thoughts:

I can never remember being greedy for richness. I can remember being really poor and not having all of my needs met. I can also remember having an abundance of love in a poor household. I can remember seeing God's truth played out in my household. My mother is a praying and faithful woman of God. I can't remember a time in my life when my mother didn't rely on prayer to address challenges. No, a desire to be rich in money and greed wasn't anything I experienced in my parent's household, nor did I introduce my children to greed. I believe that relying on God and staying in your faith journey is a sure way of getting your needs met and a sure way of staying in love with hope.

Reader's Thoughts:

~ December ~

Kindness never disappoints even when it is not reciprocated.

- December 1 -

In the end, people appreciate honest criticism far more than flattery.

Proverbs 28:23

Author's Thoughts:

Appreciating the value of honest criticism from wise resources is a journey that I intend to live in. God sends us gifts of understanding through His disciples. If you are searching for someone to disciple you and to gently introduce you to the love of Jesus, find a Jesus-sent disciple. Take time to get to know the actions and heart of your disciples.

Reader's Thoughts:

- December 2 -

Anyone who steals from his father and mother and says,
"What's wrong with that?" is no better than a murderer.
Proverbs 28:24

Author's Thoughts:

For those of you who live under rocks, let me enlighten you about the impact of drugs on our families. Drug addiction is a massive threat to our families and communities. In part, social media has resulted in parents communicating with their teenage children via electronic messages, and our children are glued to a social media outlet. This has resulted in lack of face-to-face conversations. How can a parent monitor a teenager without face time, without life discussions, without getting to know what's important to your children, or without them feeling your love through time and touch? Drugs are a "feel good" answer to feeling inadequate.

Reader's Thoughts:

- December 3 -

Greed causes fighting; trusting the Lord leads to prosperity.

Proverbs 28:25

Author's Thoughts:

Prosperity for me is God providing all of my needs. I can truly say that since I started college in 1979, God has provided all of my needs with abundance. There were times when my needs, in my mind, were not met, and those moments were filled with pity. Since 2009, I have been a single mom and God has provided all of my needs and the needs of my children. My life is simple, and my needs are few. I am hopeful and feel God's presence always.

Reader's Thoughts:

- December 4 -

Trusting a fool to convey a message is like
cutting off one's feet or drinking poison!
Proverbs 26:6

Author's Thoughts:

Trust your own message and trust that you can relay it best. Never ask someone else to communicate on your behalf unless that person has godly wisdom or you trust their thought process. Remember your communicator has your reputation wrapped in every word.

Reader's Thoughts:

- December 5 -

We can make our plans but the Lord determines our steps.

Proverbs 16:9

Author's Thoughts:

Thanks be to God for directing our steps. God can be trusted with each step. Setting goals and making plans is a structured way of living our lives and can keep us focused. We must leave room for God's plans because His plans for us do not always hold hands with our plans. Be prepared to be uncomfortable when you are carrying out God's plans for your life. Fulfilling God's plans require you to pay attention to your faith journey and the world around you.

Reader's Thoughts:

- December 6 -

Those who trust their own insight are foolish,
but anyone who walks in wisdom is safe.
Proverbs 28:26

Author's Thoughts:

Lord, I pray that our leaders walk in wisdom and not walk in their own foolish insights. I pray that our leaders lead with gentle and strong hearts. I pray that our leaders are God-focused and not self-focused. I pray that our leaders lead with integrity and honor. I pray that our leaders govern for the interest of right and not wrong. I pray that our leaders pray and listen to God's gentle voice before making decisions. I pray that our leaders are loved and that they love their families well. Amen!

Reader's Thoughts:

- December 7 -

If the godly give in to the wicked, it's like
polluting a fountain or muddying a spring.
Proverbs 25:26

Author's Thoughts:

Well, I have been guilty of muddying springs of clear water in my lifetime. In those times of weakness, I didn't think I was giving in to wicked ways, but in hindsight, that is exactly what I was doing. I still muddy the water at times, but I am honest about my actions, and I no longer try to justify wicked behavior. I am a work in progress. My faith journey might be stagnant at times, but I am determined to move forward in faith.

Reader's Thoughts:

- December 8 -

Whoever gives to the poor will lack nothing,
but those who close their eyes to poverty will be cursed.
Proverbs 28:27

Author's Thoughts:

Godly people do not close their eyes to poverty or those in need. Godly people have hearts for service because they believe and receive God's love. God's love inspires us to love mankind. Our love for mankind stimulates a need to help. Helping those in need arouses our souls..

Reader's Thoughts:

- December 9 -

Fear of the Lord is a life-giving fountain;
it offers escape from the snares of death.
Proverbs 14:27

Author's Thoughts:

My personal fear of the Lord has saved me from the snares of sin countless times. The wisdom I use to make decisions comes from God and it is because of my fear of consequences that I apply wisdom to most of my decisions. I am pleased when my actions make Jesus smile.

Reader's Thoughts:

- December 10 -

Whoever stubbornly refuse to accept criticism
will suddenly be destroyed beyond recovery.
Proverbs 29:1

Author's Thoughts:

Some criticism requires us to think before responding. We should take criticism seriously and apply a fair and sensible thought process when considering the criticism. The source of the criticism determines the degree of wisdom applied to the criticism. Just and fair criticism with a loving and gentle message is food for our souls.

Reader's Thoughts:

- December 11 -

If a ruler pays attention to liars, all his advisers will be wicked.

Proverbs 29:12

Author's Thoughts:

Liars are not undercover, their ability to lie doesn't go unnoticed by God. If you are unable to discern words and actions, liars can fool you into thinking they are telling the truth. Liars are capable of doing wicked things. Embracing the actions of a liar can result in you making silly and unwise decisions.

Reader's Thoughts:

- December 12 -

The poor and the oppressor have this in common–
the Lord gives sight to the eyes of both.
Proverbs 29:13

Author's Thoughts:

The oppressed and the oppressor both have sight, but they view and experience life from different lenses. The oppressed has lens filled with sight directed at forgiveness. The oppressor has a lens filled with sight directed towards control and disrespect. Both the oppressed and oppressor have an opportunity to enter God's kingdom through Jesus Christ. The oppressed experiences freedom in the love of Jesus Christ.

Reader's Thoughts:

- December 13 -

To discipline a child produces wisdom,
but a mother is disgraced by an undisciplined child.
Proverbs 29:15

Author's Thoughts:

I questioned my discipline style when my children became teenagers. I wasn't always consistent and I compromised my old school values too often. I always disciplined in ways that didn't demean my children, but I wasn't always firm. I didn't believe in getting physical with my children, and at times a spanking was warranted. It seems I still have a lot to learn about effective discipline because I am still inconsistent, and some would say too soft. My children have disappointed me, but I have never felt disgraced by my children.

Reader's Thoughts:

~ December 14 ~

When people do not accept divine guidance,
they run wild. But whoever obeys the law is joyful.
Proverbs 29:18

Author's Thoughts:

I can't remember a time when I haven't believed in or accepted divine guidance from God. I have always revered even the thought of Jesus. God is my hero. Jesus and His divine power saved my soul and elevated my spirit. My soul is filled with joy at all times. I never forget God's almighty powers.

Reader's Thoughts:

- December 15 -

The righteous despise the unjust; the wicked despise the godly.

Proverbs 29:27

Author's Thoughts:

If you live your life not hating or detesting anyone, the wicked will see an image of God. When you consider yourself godly, hate shouldn't enter your heart. There are people and things that we all dislike, but when our dislike turns into hate, the impact is resting on you, not the person you hate. Forgiveness is in order when hate rears its ugly head.

Reader's Thoughts:

- December 16 -

Every word of God proves true. He is a shield
to all who come to him for protection.
Proverbs 30:5

Author's Thoughts:

Lord I need and appreciate your protection. I would be clueless and weak without access to your strength and awareness. Your word is responsible for my hopeful attitude and future. I am thankful for your armor of protection. I appreciate the fact that I can depend on your unconditional love.

Reader's Thoughts:

- December 17 -

Do not add to his words, or he may rebuke you and expose you as a liar.

Proverbs 30:6

Author's Thoughts:

Understanding the word requires wisdom, study, and the Holy Spirit. Applying the word requires commitment to God's commands. Loving God and loving your neighbor is achievable through a devoted faith journey. Misrepresenting His word is wicked.

Reader's Thoughts:

- December 18 -

Who can find a virtuous and capable wife?
She is more precious than rubies.
Her husband can trust her and she will greatly enrich his life.
She brings him good, not harm, all the days of her life.
Proverbs 31:10-12

Author's Thoughts:

Women with high moral standards should pray for husbands with high moral standards. Husbands who honor, love, and appreciate good, enthusiastic, and capable wives, are a blessing to their families. Women who respect honorable husbands are jewels.

Reader's Thoughts:

- December 19 -

By wisdom the Lord founded the earth;
by understanding He created the heavens.
Proverbs 3:19

Author's Thoughts:

Pray for what you want. If wisdom intimidates you, pray for clarity. If you think you are not wise and have a desire to be wise, pray that God blesses you with wisdom and understanding so that you handle wisdom with grace. God's wisdom is clearly the foundation of this earth. With wisdom and understanding of the word, we can carry out God's plans for our lives.

Reader's Thoughts:

- December 20 -

Don't plot harm against your neighbor,

for those who live nearby trust you.

Proverbs 3:29

Author's Thoughts:

If harming your neighbor gives you any satisfaction, harming others is easy and probably rewarding in sinful ways. Violating the trust of people that love you makes you a fool. A trusting relationship is worthy of protecting and worthy of your respect.

Reader's Thoughts:

- December 21 -

My child, listen to me and do as I say,
and you will have a long, good life.
Proverbs 4:10

Author's Thoughts:

Children, listen to your godly parents. Children, learn to appreciate discipline that's meant to teach you good life lessons. Children, always consider that your parents are imperfect, and remember that their intentions and instructions are good. Children, love and respect your parents.

Reader's Thoughts:

- December 22 -

Don't even think about it; don't go that way.
Turn away and keep moving.
Proverbs 4:15

Author's Thoughts:

There are bad opportunities that are very tempting. These bad opportunities are clearly life altering and have lifelong negative consequences. The only response is to say no and run away as fast as humanly possible. If you don't turn away, you will regret the weight that saying yes will have on your life journey. If you indulge and you have a relationship with God, you will be forgiven, but God will be just and fair with His chosen ramifications.

Reader's Thoughts:

- December 23 -

The way of the righteous is like the first gleam of dawn,
which shines ever brighter until the full light of day.
Proverbs 4:18

Author's Thoughts:

Life is peaceful when your light shines bright at all times, especially as the day breaks Staying hopeful and faithful gives your light courage to shine even in the darkest hours Jesus' light is not meant to cover you, His light is meant to brighten the world one followe at a time. Be a Jesus follower who disciples through how you live your faith journey.

Reader's Thoughts:

- December 24 -

My son, obey your father's commands,
and don't neglect your mother's instruction.
Proverbs 6:20

Author's Thoughts:

This verse brings tears to my eyes because it reminds me of my father's love and my mother's compassion. Please don't take this as arrogance, but I can truly say that I can't remember a time that my parents were aware that I disobeyed or disappointed them. Yes, I disobeyed in secret, but never so careless to cause my parents pain. I am thankful for my parents and I will always honor their lives by how I live. My mom is eighty-five, she never allows the world to change her. She lives a life of dedication to God and family.

Reader's Thoughts:

- December 25 -

I, wisdom, live together with good judgement,
I know where to discover knowledge and discernment.
Proverbs 8:12

Author's Thoughts:

God, please gift your children with knowledge and discernment. God, we pray that we can live lives that are worthy of your approval. Lord, we pray that we can embrace your wisdom and apply wisdom to our decision making processes. God, we are thankful for your patience and understanding. God, please humble us in our wisdom. Amen!

Reader's Thoughts:

- December 26 -

All who fear the Lord will hate evil. Therefore,
I hate pride and arrogance, corruption and perverse speech.
Proverbs 8:13

Author's Thoughts:

Prideful people make my soul stir up concerns and make me want to protect my heart. Prideful people boast about being smart and wise. Prideful people take credit for all that they are and all that they do. Prideful people fail to see Jesus in themselves or others. Prideful people's insults don't matter. There is hope for prideful people.

Reader's Thoughts:

- December 27 -

The blessing of the Lord makes a person rich, and He adds no sorrow with it.

Proverbs 10:22

Author's Thoughts:

Do your blessings come without sorrow? God's blessings are our favor and protection. God's blessings are full of grace and mercy. God's blessings are bright and comforting. God's blessings are wonderfully timely. God's blessings inspire hope. God's blessings are promised. God's blessings save us. God's blessings turn sorrow into joy.

Reader's Thoughts:

- December 28 -

A gracious woman gains respect, but ruthless men gain only wealth.

Proverbs 11:16

Author's Thoughts:

Even in temporary defeat, a gracious woman remains kind and considerate. Men who show no compassion for women or disrespect women are misguided. If men are using their power and/or wealth to take advantage of women, it only means that they are weaker than their victims. Even if the victims remain silent about the abuse, the abusers are not unseen. God is fair and just, He sees and responds to all sin.

Reader's Thoughts:

- December 29 -

Your kindness will reward you, but your cruelty will destroy you.

Proverbs 11:17

Author's Thoughts:

Kindness never disappoints, even when it is not reciprocated. Kindness is like love, you don't wait for others to love you first, and you don't wait for others to be kind. Love and kindness should be expressed without conditions. It takes a godly person to love and be kind without conditions. Jesus provided us such a straight path for loving well and for genuine kindness.

Reader's Thoughts:

- December 30 -

Evil people get rich for the moment,
but the reward of the godly will last.
Proverbs 11:18

Author's Thoughts:

Getting rich has never been a goal of mine. When I think of rich, I think of rich in spirit, mind, and soul. I want my heart to be rich in love, kindness, forgiveness, hope, peace, compassion and consideration. I would like for God to reward me for the richness of my soul, instead of monetary richness.

Reader's Thoughts:

- December 31 -

Words alone will not discipline a servant;

the words may be understood, but they are not heeded.

Proverbs 29:19

Author's Thoughts:

Discipline requires actions and examples. If you discipline with words and not follow through with consequential actions, the purpose and impact of the discipline will be disregarded. All disciplinarians should be prepared to be flexible because effective discipline requires a position of current knowledge and commitment to applying appropriate discipline.

Reader's Thoughts:

Author's Final Thoughts:

Life is brief and sometimes bewildering. I pray that you can find proper wisdom and contentment through all circumstances. My personal experience is that you can find true wisdom by trusting in God and in His ways. Fearing God and obeying His commands leads to a wise heart. I have learned to dance while mourning.

Peace be with you always!